The Dancing Man

Robert Byron

THE DANCING MAN

iUniverse books may be ordered through booksellers or by contacting:

iUniverse
1663 Liberty Drive
Bloomington, IN 47403
www.iuniverse.com
1-800-Authors (1-800-288-4677)

Because of the dynamic nature of the Internet, any web addresses or links contained in this book may have changed since publication and may no longer be valid. The views expressed in this work are solely those of the author and do not necessarily reflect the views of the publisher, and the publisher hereby disclaims any responsibility for them.

Any people depicted in stock imagery provided by Thinkstock are models, and such images are being used for illustrative purposes only. Certain stock imagery © Thinkstock.

ISBN: 978-1-4917-3861-0 (sc)
ISBN: 978-1-4917-3862-7 (e)

Library of Congress Control Number: 2014910959

Print information available on the last page.

iUniverse rev. date: 02/09/2015

Contents

Introduction

For those of us who grew up in the shadows of the Greatest Generation, the scope of the WWII conflict and the clarity of the victory remain a marvel. But as the shadows of that generation recede, the generations that followed have had challenges of their own. Korea, Vietnam, lunar landings, nuclear threats, terrorist threats and political upheaval are on the list. But despite the contemporary challenges, the Greatest Generation remains a hard act to follow.

This account traces the journey of an individual born too late for military service in WWII but in time for the Korean conflict. It is a journey that spans the Cold War, the Cuban missile crisis, the space race, the lunar landing, the digital age and terrorist threats. It traces a life whose passage through institutions like the Catholic Church, Marine Corps, family life, political skirmishes and different working environments are shared by many. But dancing sets us apart. More than anything else, dancing was a common thread of family cohesion and beyond. The dance connection eventually spanned folk, country, ballroom and west coast swing. To this day, dancing remains a stabilizing factor, outlet for exercise and a socializing force. It does so despite divorce, the passing of my former wife, and the passing of three of my four children.

I was three when FDR was elected, five when Social Security became law and thirty-five when Johnson signed Medicare into law. I feel I have come full circle -from the depression thirties and post WWII boom to recessions and a world in the throes of government upheavals and economic challenges.

This journey begins in Germantown, a Philadelphia suburb and covers a life spanning most of the 20th and early 21st.centuries. It will take the reader through transitions ranging from life in a religious order to the Marine Corps and to subsequent associations with aerospace, local government and public schools. It is a life in which professional pursuits have been interwoven with a continuous connection to the dance.

In the late sixties, Peggy Lee, a leading songstress of the era, popularized a song called "Is That All There Is?" The lyrics addressed the downside of life but offered dancing as an offset. Although I don't subscribe to the nihilism of the lyrics, I related to the pragmatism of the advice. I also relate to the life validating philosophies of General Douglas MacArthur and noted Holocaust survivor and psychiatrist Viktor Frankl. MacArthur advocated living each day as if you were going to live forever. Frankl offered work as a recipe for happiness if the work was what you really wanted to do.

In some ways, the accounting of a life's journey might be considered a modern day take-off on a 15th century morality play. Those plays traced events in the life of a typical individual, known as Everyman, as he journeyed through life. The only thing Everyman can carry forward into the next life is his record of accomplishments. It is my hope that this account provides a template for readers to assess their own lives and the legacy they will bequeath to their successors. Given our extended life span, we have more time than ever to enhance our record. Let's not waste it.

Robert J Byron

Chapter 1

THE THIRTIES

The thirties were lean years. The market crash put the damper on the high flying twenties. The depression thirties followed. Unemployment, hunger, soup kitchens and mortgage foreclosures were at an all time high. Even the forces of nature added to the misery with the erosion of midwest farmland. The stagnation of the economy cast a pall over the nation while fascist states like Germany and Italy were busy preparing for wartime adventurism. Japan was also translating a Tanaka doctrine of a greater Far East co-prosperity sphere with its military penetration of China and Korea. Franklin Roosevelt's 1932 Democratic victory signaled the beginning of national will to make an economic turnaround. Keynesian economics were put into play. Our economic pump would be primed with government spending. In his 1933 inaugural address, FDR had it right – "the only thing we have to fear is fear itself"

Franklin Roosevelt had his hands full trying to overcome a domestic crisis of twenty-five percent unemployment. But his inaugural speech immortalized the uniqueness of the times and gave hope to millions. His famous words –"this generation of Americans has a rendezvous with destiny" were prophetic.

On the brighter side, Prohibition was repealed, Social Security enacted and the American labor movement was growing. The Works Project Administration (WPA) was pumping money into local economies and putting men to work. Many public buildings and infrastructure-related tasks were completed. A Civilian Conservation Corps (CCC) was putting

1

idle young men work. The Keynesian economic model had taken hold. But there was still a lot of suffering. Soil erosion in the mid-West was forcing farmers to give up their farms and head west – a tragedy that John Steinbeck recounted in his classic Grapes of Wrath. War clouds over Europe were beginning to stimulate America's manufacturing sector. Hitler was re-arming despite the Versailles Treaty. But Britain's Prime Minister, Neville Chamberlain, after meeting with Hitler in1938 assured Britons and the world there would be peace in our times even as the Sudetenland was annexed to Germany. Winston Churchill was skeptical.

Germantown

Germantown is located in northwest Philadelphia and should be included in any historic tour of Philadelphia. It was settled in 1683 by German Mennonites under the leadership of Daniel Pastorius, a Quaker who brought members of his sect with him at the invite of William Penn. Penn, himself a Quaker, was granted a charter for Pennsylvania two years earlier by Britain's Charles II. Penn and the Quaker influence are visible to this day. One familiar Quaker landmark is The Friends School on School House Lane built in 1689.

Germantown was also the site of a battle between British and American forces in 1777. The battle didn't go too well for General Washington. What began as a surprise attack on the British to slow their advance on downtown Philadelphia turned into a rout for Washington's forces. Foggy weather, confusion in the ranks of both sides and the stubborn resistance of some British troops holed up in the home of Pennsylvania jurist John Chew forced Washington to retreat. Some of America's ablest generals were engaged in this campaign including Nathaniel Greene and Henry Knox. The boldness of Washington's attack, however, like his successes a few months earlier at Princeton and Trenton, heartened the French and encouraged them to support our revolutionary efforts.

Looking Back

Looking back on our modest, 2 story row house on Bringhurst Street, I would consider my family and our neighborhood middle class. The coming war would bump us up a notch on the middle class ladder.

We were renters like most others in our neighborhood but the homes, though small, were comfortable and just right for a family of four. It had a small front porch and a small backyard. We even had a cellar that provided space for coal storage, doing the laundry, playing darts, shooting BB guns and practicing on a punching bag. But the depression thirties would soon transition into more prosperous times as war clouds gathered in Europe. Demands for American goods were growing. European woes spelled better economic times for the US.

But until the war in Europe took off, the thirties were a time of financial struggle for most. Few escaped the daily scramble to make a buck. Fortunately, family life was much tighter and families stuck together including the extended family of aunts and uncles, cousins and nephews. My immediate family circle consisted of Mom and Dad and brother Joe. I was born in May 1930 and my brother Joe came along a year later. We were both born in the Germantown Hospital just two blocks from our house. My mother, called Margaret by her sisters and Peg by Dad, had three sisters and a brother. Anna, Rita, Dorothy and Vincent. All were married and lived nearby. Aunt Anna, in fact, lived right across the street. Dad, or Pat as he was called, had a younger brother, Mike, and two sisters, Agnes and Margaret. Uncle Mike was a bachelor and didn't seem to have a fixed residence. Dad's sisters, both married, lived some miles away in Tacony a suburb of northeast Philadelphia not far from the Delaware River. Mom's brother Vince had four children - Vince, Mary, Dottie and Ruthie. I saw Grandpa Finn frequently but saw Grandpa Byron only occasionally. I never saw either of my grandmothers.

Grandpa Finn's Influence

Grandpa Finn, my mother's father, lived about two miles from us and would join us for supper about once a week. He was a weekly dinner guest at each daughter's home. He was living alone in the large home he owned on Church Lane, the same home he used to raise his family. He seemed to enjoy the company these family dinners provided. Apart from the little my mother told me about her father, I never knew much about Grandpa Finn's wife. I knew he was born in this country and that his

3

lineage included a highly regarded Catholic priest who did missionary work in China and would later preside at my wedding..

Grandpa Finn, or Gramps as we called him, had more to do with introducing Joe and me to our country's history than anyone else. Gramps who was able to retire in his fifties due to the financial bonanza of his funeral supply business during the flu epidemic of 1918. He loved to walk and had a unique spring in his step which Joe and I liked to imitate. We took frequent hikes to downtown Philadelphia about seven miles from home. Keeping up with Gramps was not easy. When we got to the center of the city, we would visit Independence Hall where the Declaration of Independence was signed in 1776, Carpenter's Hall where the First Continental Congress met in 1774 and Betsy Ross' house where our first flag was designed. We would take in the Liberty Bell and the many monuments to Philadelphia's foremost citizen and one of the nation's founders, Benjamin Franklin. Franklin's talent and genius as an inventor, scientist, political leader, businessman, publisher, writer and ambassador were recognized and appreciated at home and abroad. He was Philadelphia's most prominent citizen. His was among that remarkably capable band of leaders who brought the nation to fruition - Washington, Adams, Jefferson, Madison and Hamilton. Franklin's role in securing a French alliance was instrumental in securing America's final victory at Yorktown in 1781.

At the end of these jaunts, Joe and I always looked forward to stopping by the Horn and Hardart automat for a piece of pie and a glass of milk. Taking the subway home afterwards was always a welcome relief. These downtown jaunts, though a favorite with Gramps, were an endurance contest for Joe and me.

Lean Times and Respites

Understandably, the thirties were financially difficult for most. With over 25% of the population struggling to get on a payroll, times were tough. I never thought much of it then but stuffing cardboard in your shoes to cover up the holes until your parents could afford new shoes or get old ones mended was not uncommon. Even kids were doing whatever they could to earn money. I remember being paid for posing for a local artist. Albert Hampton. This artist lived up the street and was commissioned by the Saturday Evening Post to do a portrait for its cover. The portrait he created was that of a young boy and girl bowing to each other as a prelude to a dance. I posed with Doris Aherne another six year old who lived on the same street. We were both dressed in formal dance wear - I wore black short pants, a Buster Brown collar and patent leather shoes; Doris wore a bouffant dress, patent leather shoes and wore her hair in long curls. We were both bowing to each other but with our tongues stuck out while a dance master was glancing back over his shoulder with a disapproving look. I forget how much we were paid but whatever it was seemed like a small fortune to me. The portrait appeared on the May 23, 1936 issue of the Saturday Evening Post.

The following year, Walt Disney's classic *Snow White and the Seven Dwarfs* animated movie made its grand opening at the Germantown theatre on Germantown Avenue. I remember going to see it. The cost for a child's ticket at the time was 10 cents. Two years later, the Wizard of Oz hit the screen and everyone had to see it. In fact, the local movie theatre hosted a special showing during regular school hours just for kids from the Immaculate Conception. Our entire 4th grade class was part of a long line of students including nuns walking several blocks down Chelton Avenue to the Walton theatre. I enjoyed singing the hit tune of that film, Somewhere Over the Rainbow. I sang it so much my father took me for a singing audition at WCAU, a Philadelphia radio station that held a weekly amateur hour. Unfortunately, when it was my turn to sing, I opened my mouth and nothing came out. It was the first time I ever experienced stage fright. I had let my family down and really felt bad. It was a humbling and embarrassing experience.

We did a lot of things to make money during those lean depression days including collecting old newspapers and selling them to the junkman, running errands for neighbors and selling magazines. Besides Liberty magazine, my best seller was the Woman's Home Companion. I made a commission on every copy I sold. There were also prize incentives for increasing the number of subscribers. I won my share. Some of the money I earned I shared with Mom. Sometimes it helped put a meal on the table. I felt good when I could contribute. I also had ear problems that I knew meant added expense for Mom and Dad. I had four mastoid operations on the same ear over the space of two years. These meant operations and hospital stay plus doctor visits afterwards. My only pleasant memories of those hospital stays were the Dixie cups my parents brought me when they visited. The lids on these ice cream cups had pictures of movie stars. I always left the hospital with a small collection of movie star photos.

Much of my life from the mid-thirties and for the next eight years was centered on schooling at the Immaculate Conception grammar school where nuns of the Immaculate Heart order taught. Catholic education was a solid, no-nonsense affair. The school day went from 8:30 am to 4 pm weekdays. There were the seasonal breaks and holidays plus the usual activities that went with the seasons. Fall meant wrestling matches and king-on-the-hill contests in the leaf piles, making pipes out of hollowed-out chestnuts, roller skating, roller hockey and riding skatos (skateboards) that we made ourselves. With winter came snow, sledding and snowball fights. There were some hilly streets that were great for downhill sledding. Usually there were enough cars to catch a ride back up by hanging on a bumper. The snow ball fights were fun especially when the snow was wet enough to make heavier and more compact balls. Spring meant baseball and shooting marbles. Summer meant getting doused with water from fire plug sprinklers, snow cones with flavored ice, Jack and Jill ice cream and swimming at the Boys Club.

Towards the end of the decade, something else was in the air – war. Ready reminders of the bombings and killings in China came in the form of the war cards enclosed in bubble gum wrappers. The cards displayed gruesome pictures of civilian casualties and other war related pictures. My bedroom walls were plastered with photos of bombers, fighter planes and military uniforms from different countries. One of our favorite games was war maneuvers. We would stake out objectives in different parts of nearby woods, arm ourselves with our BB guns and take off on our missions. I would even write out orders for others to follow. But come supper time, war fighting gave way to our favorite radio programs like Jack Armstrong, the Lone Ranger, the Green Hornet and the Shadow.

Grandpa Finn's Legacy

Grandpa Finn left his mark on all of us. He was a motivator who walked the talk. Thrift, hard work, determination and independence were his core values. His early retirement gave him time to communicate his beliefs to his grandchildren. His influence on his daughters remained strong especially when it came to smoking. He disapproved of women smoking. His daughters, all of whom smoked, would never dare smoke in his presence. On his weekly dinner rounds to each of his daughters' homes, Aunt Anna and Mom would generally find an excuse to visit one another during Gramps' visit for dinner. Getting out of the house on the pretense for borrowing a cup of flour or something else was the usual cover for a getting a smoking break. As for himself, Grandpa smoked a pipe and an occasional cigar. Everyone admired his thrifty life style. To retire in one's fifties was a remarkable achievement in those days. But Grandpa Finn was in the right business at the right time. His funeral supply business was operating at the height of flu epidemic of 1918 that claimed hundreds of thousands of American lives. Gramps was in the right business at the right time.

Mom and Dad

Mom was born in Germantown, attended a Catholic grammar school and had a year or so of commercial school. She married soon after and was a stay-at-home housewife. She stood just under five feet, had black hair, hazel eyes and wore glasses. She had a piano and loved to play it. Although she read music, she could play anything by ear. A bundle of energy, she was always helping others and never seemed to have an idle moment. Her sisters usually looked up to her because she was the oldest and because she assumed the mother's role when Gramps second wife left him.

Mom kept a tidy home, made good stew, pork and sour kraut, and apple pie. I loved her apple pie although she thought her crust was too soggy. But that's the way I liked it. She also had a temper. When she got mad, she threw whatever was in her hand or nearby. I got good at ducking. When I laughed because she missed, it made her madder. But her temper explosions were not that frequent and were over quickly.

Dad was born in Orange, New Jersey. Although Grandpa Byron was born Ireland, all his children were born in the US. These included Dad's brother Mike and sisters Margaret and Agnes. I only got to see Grandpa Byron when he came to our house for an occasional Sunday dinner. I remember his thick, Irish brogue and how hard it was for me to understand what he was saying. He would eat European style, with a knife in his right hand and a fork in the other never switching. He was good natured and enjoyed talking about his experiences. He passed away in the late 1930's of stomach cancer. I never knew his wife or anything about her. In fact, I never saw or knew anything about either of my grandmothers.

Dad was slender, average height, thinning blond hair and blue eyes. He was a neat dresser, usually wore a shirt and tie and kept his shoes shined. Dad had a mechanical and technical aptitude that he used to advantage in working for Philco Radio and later at the Frankfort Arsenal. He was always available to help neighbors with radio repairs and enjoyed entering puzzle contests that the Philadelphia Bulletin offered in its Sunday edition. He won several prizes. He also liked to study the manuals on the characteristics of new machinery like the Brown and Sharp automatic screw machines. He was also proficient in the use of a slide rule. Dad also enjoyed his beer on weekends, singing to Mom's piano accompaniment and playing the spoons and the Jews harp. Although I never saw Dad dance, I think he might have been a Fred Astaire type.

Uncle Mike

Uncle Mike was about the same size as Dad but more muscular with black curly hair and a year-round suntan from working as a caddy on the golf links. Joe and I liked to ask him to make a muscle which was about the size of an orange. We also liked the cheesecake he brought home when he came for supper or stayed overnight. He had a gift for storytelling and a musical bent that included playing the guitar and tap dancing.

Family Entertainment

When the whole family got together, which was frequently, we had our own entertainment group. Mom would play the piano, Dad would sing through a rolled up newspaper. His favorite songs included "It's Only a Shanty in Old Shanty Town", "Dear Doctor John","Peg O' My Heart","Danny Boy", "Whispering" and the "Downtown Strutters Ball". He also enjoyed the Ink Spots and the Mills Brothers.

Gramp's contribution to our musical group included songs sung with accompanying gestures. He sung "Lightning Bug" with arm motions suggesting plucking lightning bugs from the air. Uncle Mike would play the guitar and tap dance. Joe and I would sing. Joe was also displaying instrumental talent and a gift for comedy.

We created a stage environment for our entertainment nights by using part of our dining room. We would draw back the drapes separating the living room and dining room for theatrical effect while Mom provided musical background on the piano.

It was a golden age for radio. We would all sit around in the living room listening to our Philco radio and enjoying such radio greats as Bob (Pepsodent) Hope, Gracie Allen, George Burns, Fibber McGee and Molly, Major Bowes and Charlie McCarthy.

In the late thirties, the after dinner talk among the grown-ups began centering on labor unions, Father Coughlin, Adolph Hitler, the Jews, Mussolini and the economy. It was obvious that the military posturing in Europe and the German invasion of Poland were increasing the demand for American food and manufactured goods. With the Polish aggression, England and France declared war on Germany. But France would soon capitulate and England would need all the help it could get. It seems this generation of Americans was going to rendezvous with destiny after all.

Chapter Two

THE FORTIES

The forties reflected the "rendezvous with destiny" prophecy of FDR's 1933 inaugural speech. It was at Sunday dinner about 4PM at our house when the first news of the Japanese attack on Pearl Harbor was blared over the radio. We were shocked, dismayed and angered. I remember asking Mom if I could smash a teacup that was made in Japan. Looking at the broken pieces helped relieve some of my anger although it didn't make sense economically. In the coming decade would witness our recovery from Pearl Harbor and the triumph of our arms throughout North Africa, Italy, Europe, and the Pacific. The atom bomb would introduce a terror stalemate and a prolonged Cold War with the Soviets. The GI Bill would usher in unprecedented housing and educational opportunities for millions of ex-GIs. And, I would find myself drawn to teaching as a member of a religious teaching order, the Brothers of the Christian Schools.

WWII Years

The war improved the financial lot of my family and most of the country dramatically. We were the arsenal of democracy. Dad took a good, permanent job at the Frankfort Arsenal, a munitions manufacturer. He would work there until emphysema forced his retirement and resulted in his early death. But the war affected everyone not just those in uniform or working in defense industries. The whole tempo and mood of the country changed. After the economic doldrums of the thirties,

America was energized. All of us were all caught up in the excitement of the war. A new energy surged throughout the country. Neighborhood kids were caught up in playing war games. We talked about going on maneuvers. I would write out orders for my gang of would-be warriors specifying objectives in nearby Wister Woods as well as the necessary logistic support like water, sticks and stones. I felt well-armed with my Daisy Defender BB gun and BB pistol. It wasn't long before the Marine exploits on Guadalcanal captured my imagination. I don't know how many times I read Richard Tregaskis' Guadalcanal Diary.

This was also an era of ration stamps. Red stamps were for meat, blue stamps for canned goods and white stamps for dairy. Gasoline was also rationed. You needed a special sticker in the window of your car indicating your gas priority. Uncle John had such a card because he worked for the Post Office and used his car for special delivery. With all the rationing I never had a sense of deprivation. I think we ate better during the war years than in the thirties. I worked as a delivery boy and behind the counter for Flowers' Grocery store and had access to more food than most. Also contributing to our food supply were the victory gardens. Vacant plots of land were available for growing vegetables. Families were quick to take advantage of the opportunity to grow their own vegetables. Over the next couple years we would grow our own corn, tomatoes and string beans. It made us feel like small farmers.

Once the pace of the war years settled in, a new prosperity was visible. It even meant we could afford to vacation at Atlantic City or Wildwood, New Jersey. We would usually squeeze into Uncle John's car to make the trip. Joe and I would sit in the rumble seat, something we really enjoyed. Whenever we neared the coast we could smell the difference. The salt air of the Atlantic Ocean felt good to breathe. The very sight of the ocean was always overpowering to me.

Taking an out-of-state vacation was practically unheard of during the thirties. Our vacations were usually limited to week-end picnics at local parks and an annual school bus outing to amusement parks like Willow Grow or Woodside. But now we were vacationing at the seashore. Dad still didn't have a car but we would pile into Uncle John's and away we'd go.

Strolls on the boardwalk, visits to Steele Pier, buying salt water taffy, sending postcards to relatives and friends, eating Maria pork rolls, playing skeetball, swimming in the ocean and sunning on the beach – these were all new adventures for us, things the new prosperity made possible. Popular songs at the time included "Pistol Packing Mama" and the "Acheson, Topeka and the Santa Fe". We were in Wildwood on August 6, 1945 when we heard news of the atomic bomb drop on Hiroshima. A week later, another bomb was dropped on Nagasaki. A month later, the war ended.

The depression and especially the war introduced the American people to a mobility that many had never experienced. There was also an earlier exodus in the thirties caused by the mid-west farmland drought captured so well in Steinbeck's Grapes of Wrath. There was also the job search by the unemployed. But the war brought about massive relocations due to military service and defense jobs. People moved west for military training and jobs in aircraft factories. Military personnel were transferring to different parts of the country and getting to different parts of the world, parts they would never have seen except for the war. People were discovering life beyond their own neighborhoods.

However, the war also had a stiff price tag. Too many windows in our neighborhood were filled with gold and blue star banners. The gold indicated killed in action; the blue, wounded. I wrote a lot of letters to my older friends in the service keeping them current with neighborhood news. I generally concluded each letter asking for war souvenirs. By the end of the war, I had a Japanese rifle and bayonet, an antique French revolver, German medals, German officer caps and swastikas, an American bayonet and a helmet liner. I also had enough American insignia and overseas caps to outfit our own little band of neighborhood warriors in-waiting.

In 1944 I completed grammar school at the Immaculate Conception. Without studying too hard, I got good grades. I had been an altar boy and a lieutenant on the Safety Squad. In my graduation year I was recognized for excellent scholarship, perfect attendance and awarded the American Legion medal. I also won a partial scholarship to La Salle High, a college prep high school taught by the Brothers of the Christian

Schools. Were it not for Dad's Frankfort Arsenal job and my partial scholarship, La Salle would probably been out of reach financially.

I met my future wife, Bernice, around this time while walking with some friends to a movie on a cold winter night. It was a chance encounter. As we passed some row houses on School House Lane, I noticed a pretty teenage girl through the living room window of one of the houses. I was struck by her beauty and asked my friends to wait as I knocked on the door. When Bernie answered, I introduced myself. In the brief exchange that followed I learned that she was attending Little Flower, a Catholic high school for girls. I got her phone number. This was the start of our relationship. As I said good-bye with a promise to call her soon, I could hear the strains of Vaughn Monroe singing "Let it Snow" coming from her radio. That "soon" turned out to be several years but it concluded with our marriage.

I was now attending La Salle High School. During my sophomore year I came under the influence of Brother Daniel. He was my Latin teacher, ran the school's photo lab and was an impressive athlete. He was a poster boy for attracting candidates to the religious life. He would single out students likely to fit the profile of a religious teacher. I was one of them. Comparable proselytizing efforts took place in all the schools run by the Brothers. Some forty high school age students were then in training at the Brothers' junior novitiate in Maryland. As part of the process, Brother Daniel met my parents and took me and one other student on a trip to the Brothers' training center for high school level candidates in Maryland. The name of the site was Ammendale just about about 10 miles from Washington DC. It gave us a first hand look at the facilities. I was impressed. Now I had the information necessary for some really serious decision-making. While there, we took in the sights and sounds of the nation's capitol. It was my first visit.

Ammendale was 400 acre site with a Beltsville, Maryland mailing address. . It was the training center for the Brothers' high school recruits, the site of their senior Novitiate and center for retired Brothers. Some joked that the name was based on all the "amens" added to the many prayers said there. In reality, the site was named for Admiral David Ammen, a retired naval officer who served with distinction during the Civil War. He donated the property to the Brothers in 1881. The community was self-sufficient in many ways. It had its own dairy cow and a chicken farm, wheat fields and honey bees. The site was rich in oak and pine trees and had two major buildings housing its population including classrooms, chapels, dormitories and refectories. It had a swimming pool, outdoor handball and basketball courts and playing fields for baseball and football. When we returned from this orientation, it was time for serious soul-searching for me and my parents. Even Aunt Anna got into the act.

I was captivated with the idea of standing in front of a classroom like Brother Daniel, wearing a black robe and teaching. I also saw it as a way of doing something as dramatic as going off to war. The German prisoners-of-war housed at a National Guard Armory next to La Salle High were a constant reminder of a victory soon to be at hand. I would watch them use our high school football field to play soccer and I would watch a German-speaking Brother converse with them. Prospects for my being involved in the war had dropped to zero. From the age of ten, I was obsessed with joining the Marines and fighting in the Pacific. Richard Tregaskis' Guadacanal Diary was my bible. I couldn't wait until I was old enough to join. So when prospects for engaging in the war grew dim, my energies shifted to another dramatic outlet. I felt I was old enough to do something significant on my own. I thought joining the Brothers would be an adventure I needed.

"Margaret, you are making a big mistake letting a 15 year old boy join a religious order. He doesn't know anything about life. He's too young to make such a big decision." Aunt Anna was dead set against my going away to join a religious order. She felt I should at least finish high school before I made such a big step. I know Mom and Dad must have had mixed emotions but I was persistent. I think I wore Mom down. As far as I could tell, Mom was the real decision maker. So, in the middle of my sophomore year, with a lot of mixed family emotions, I said goodbye to Mom, Dad and brother Joe. There were hugs, kisses and a lump in my throat. With Brother Daniel at the wheel, I left Germantown and drove off to Ammendale.

Looking back, I'm sure the education I got was the best. There were few distractions to my study regimen. Classes were small, six to ten students at most. The teachers were excellent. I acquired a sense of self-discipline and Christian values. I also developed a lifelong love of learning. But I also lost something, perhaps a too-early loss of a close family connection.

St Jean Baptists de la Salle

By the time I enrolled at La Salle High, the Brothers of the Christian Schools had been on the American educational scene for some hundred years. This religious teaching order was founded in the late seventeenth century by St.John Baptiste de la Salle. He was born to a wealthy French family, well educated and highly regarded within the Catholic Church hierarchy. He understood the unmet educational needs of those not fortunate enough to be born into a wealthy or aristocratic family. So he resigned his church position and, with his own wealth, established one of the world's first free schools for youth and adults. He also established a religious teaching order to lead the learning process. At the time his schools were opening in France, the Quakers were opening theirs in Germantown. Some fifty years later, Benjamin Franklin would open a public school in Philadelphia to meet the educational needs of neglected city children.

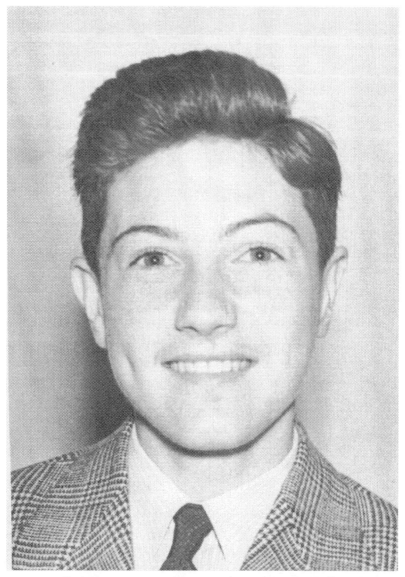

Bob Byron at age 15... a sophomore at La Salle
High School in Philadelphia, Pennsylvania

Free schooling for both youth and adults in Europe was a radical concept
when it was first introduced. Until then, education in France as elsewhere
was the preserve of the aristocracy, the clergy and the wealthy. But with
a new band of teachers, Saint Jean Baptists de la Salle established schools

and provided free instruction in basic skills, sciences, arts, trades and religion to those who not otherwise have the opportunity. His schools and methods spread throughout Europe and around the world. His innovations included the segregation of students by learning abilities and providing instruction in the spoken language of the day rather than Latin.

Ammendale

In 1845, the Brothers opened their first US school in Baltimore. Within a century, two thousand Brothers would be teaching at a hundred schools across the country. Instructional levels ranged from college, university and high schools to military academies, trade schools, correctional institutions and orphanages. To fill their ranks, the Brothers relied on the recruiting power of their own example. Since a Brother's life was immersed in study, teaching, students and prayer, candidates were expected to be up to the task. In my eyes, Brother Daniel was the perfect model as well as my sponsor.

Christian Brothers Training and Retirement
Center in Ammendale, Maryland

Ammendale was the headquarters, training center and retirement home for Brothers of the Baltimore District, a district that included states on the eastern seaboard. Referred to as the Mother House, the main structure was the center piece. This structure was an impressive four story, red-bricked building which included dining halls, a large kitchen, a chapel, study halls, dormitories for senior novices and individual rooms for retired Brothers. The junior novices were housed in a separate four story building that housed classrooms, a study hall, a chapel, recreation hall and dormitories.

These structures were set back about a quarter mile from the main highway. Trees lined both sides of the road leading to the main building. There the road ended with a circular driveway surrounding a large statue of St. John Baptiste de la Salle. There was also a small chapel and a cemetery situated some distance from the Mother House. Many Brothers who began their religious life at Ammendale ended it there as well.

Religious Life Economics

Brothers, including senior novices, took vows of poverty, chastity and obedience. In return for dedicating their life to the Order's teaching mission.. Life's essentials were provided – food, clothing, shelter, medical and dental care, continuing education and even care of one's parents if needed. Looking back, I marvel at the money management that sustained such a successful network of schools. Tuitions and donations were the primary sources of income reflecting the value that parents and graduates placed on the quality of instruction. Christian Brothers and the Jesuits were the leading teaching professionals for the Catholic Church. There was a healthy rivalry between the two.

Aunt Anna, Brother Robert and his mother, Margaret (from left to right)

Patrick Byron (father), Brother Robert, John
O'Donnell (uncle), Joe Byron (brother), and cousins
Jack and Bobby O'Donnell (from left to right)

There was a great financial advantage in having religious professionals dedicate their lives to teaching without concern for pay. Salaries are normally a major portion of a school budget. In this case, it was like having an army without having to meet a payroll. In return for dedicating their lives to teaching, all living expenses were provided. Brothers were free to pursue their studies, teaching and religious life without the distractions of a wife, children, mortgages, parents and living expenses.

Ammendale was practically self-sufficient. Some of the Brothers' hired-hands included farmers and a cook. Cows, pigs and chickens were raised and wheat was grown. As junior novices we helped with the grain harvest. In winter, we took to the woods with axes and saws to clear out dead trees. We also helped tend a bee colony and collected the honey.

Looking Back

When I first arrived at Ammendale, I was homesick. I felt especially lonely at night when I lay half- awake listening to the distant wail of a train whistle and wondering if I made the right choice. But the homesickness feeling soon passed.

Without a doubt, my education at Ammendale was extraordinarily good. My classes were small, about six to a class – that's right, six. This was tantamount to private instruction by some of the best teachers the Brothers could assign. The junior novitiate was the incubator for the order's future teachers. Study distractions were practically non-existent. Everything was done on schedule - class work, studies, sports, chores, sleeping, eating and praying. My academic regimen included English, Literature, US and World History, Geometry, Algebra, Chemistry, Biology, Physics, Latin, French and Religion. In your junior year you could choose between continuing Latin and French or shifting to advanced Algebra and Trigonometry. I chose Latin and French. Brother Basil who had spent several years teaching in French-speaking Quebec took me under his wing and did much to develop my French language skills. When the French-speaking Inspector General of our Institute visited Ammendale, I was selected to deliver a welcoming speech in French on behalf of the junior novices.

"Nous autres, les petits novices, avons ete attire a la vie religieuse par l'exemple des Freres qui nous faisaint les classes….." We, the junior novices, were attracted to the religious life by the example of the Brothers who taught us…It was quite an honor thanks to Brother Basil. He was also our choir master and organist. Our performance as a choral group, especially during Holy Week when Gregorian chant dominated, came close to matching that of the world reknowned Monks of Solesme, .

You could not find a more qualified and dedicated faculty. All held advanced degrees and had taught in high schools and colleges from Philadelphia, Pittsburgh and Baltimore to Washington DC, Quebec and Nicaragua. In Nicaragua, because of the heat, the Brothers wore a white robe instead of black.

Our progress as students was a matter of public record twice a month. While assembled in our study hall, referred to as the Common room, our school director, Brother Henry, would publicly review our academic progress. He would also preside over a unique ritual known as the Advertisement of Defects. This exercise called for each of us taking turns kneeling in front of the entire student body with our arms outstretched. We would ask fellow novices to announce publicly any actions on our part that were distracting or against the rules.

"My very dear brothers, I beseech you to have the charity to advertise me of my defects so that knowing them I may correct myself with the grace of God." With this request, fellow junior novices would rise and announce any infraction of the rules or distracting conduct.

"It seems to me, my very dear Robert that you sometimes fail to give the signal before talking to fellow novices in the hallways". Silence was a hallmark of the religious life and not always easy to maintain. There was no talking between classes, between buildings, or in the refectory or chapel. If speaking was necessary, it was preceded by a verbal signal. The initiator would say "Live Jesus in our hearts" and the one spoken to would answer "Forever". Forgetting this preamble was a common error.

Other common faults included lack of modesty of the eyes or making too much noise when rising from a desk in the Common room. Modesty of eyes was a discipline that required us to keep our eyes either downcast or focused on where we were going so as to keep distractions to a minimum. We were expected to imitate the lives of the saints.

Although our academic regimen was strong, our physical development was also attended through participation in a variety of sports including touch football, baseball, handball, basketball and swimming. The swimming pool was outdoors and used only during the summer months. I especially liked the pool having been on the La Salle High swimming team briefly before leaving for Ammendale. I also liked handball. We were expected to take our athletic talent to its highest level since our teaching responsibilities would also include oversight of sports. Some junior novices were star athletes and would have easily made varsity- level positions in basketball and baseball. Red Hawley, although short, was a whiz on the basketball court and baseball field. Another junior novice from Pittsburgh could hit a baseball as far as most professional players.

We also got to stage and participate in plays. I remember my role as Teddy Roosevelt in Arsenic and Old Lace. We also got to attend the operatic delights of Gilbert and Sullivan musicals like the HMS Pinafore, the Mikado and the Pirates of Penzance. These quality performances were put on by our Washington DC brothers who were attending Catholic University. Their memorable performances were heightened by the necessity for them to assume female roles..

We ate well. Our milk was so fresh we could almost tell by the taste where the cows were grazing. We had a temperamental but excellent cook whose chicken would melt in your mouth. I don't know how many times Charlie the cook threatened to quit only to be placated somehow by the facility Director.

Time was never wasted, even when taking our meals. Meals were normally taken in silence except for the book reading. A different book was read aloud at each meal, each junior novice taking turns reading at the sound of a bell. If someone stumbled on a word, the Director would correct him. Everyone got to read but the better readers were generally favored with a longer reading time before the bell sounded. It was an excellent exercise in effective oral reading. It exposed us to interesting material beyond the scope of required classroom reading. After each meal we would gather in groups of six or so for a 20-30 minute walk. Each group was led by a faculty Brother and our discussion would center on what was just read. The only ones excused from this exercise were those assigned to do the dishes.

The Ammendale environment was totally suited to its mission. Its setting stimulated the imagination. I can remember getting so caught up in our study of the Civil War that about four just took off on a mid-winter day and headed towards Virginia. "On to Richmond" was our mantra. As it got dark, we realized how far we had wandered from our religious preserve. We had to knock on a stranger's door and ask to use a phone. We were about ten miles from Ammendale. Fortunately, the joy of knowing we were safe overshadowed the Director's distraught over our disappearance. A Brother drove out and picked us up. The prodigal sons had returned and were just in time for supper.

We had our share of light moments. Like the time we discovered the top of a beautiful pine tree outside our building missing. It didn't take long to realize that the beautifully decorated Christmas tree in the chapel was the missing top. Our creative sacristan, Jack Greed from West Catholic High thought nothing was too good for Jesus.

Another memorable though unsightly incident was the garbage can debacle. Carrying a 40-50 gallon metal container with the liquid and solid remains of the day's meals – oatmeal, chicken parts, fat trimmings and coffee grinds – was usually a two man effort each taking one of the side handles. I'll never know what made me think I could carry that can on my shoulder by myself but I did. In attempting to hoist the container up on my shoulder, I lost my grip and the container went upside down over my head. When the Director saw and smelled my condition, I was given permission to take a shower at once. Needless to say, that attempt at a show of strength was never repeated.

Hours not spent in the classroom, study hall, playing fields or with chores were spent in the chapel and religious exercises. Everything we did was within a framework of rules, regulations and set schedules. Everything we did was considered God's will. Every one was here of their own free will. Everyone was consumed with a desire to serve the Church as a Christian Brother. Daily mass, meditation, Stations of the Cross, the rosary, Gregorian chant and religious readings were integral to the life. Silence was the order of the day except during class or recreation. The need for oversight or supervision was practically non-existent. We were a self-motivated breed.

We did, however, get some welcome breaks from this rigid routine. It came in the form of an unexpected free day. Our religious mentors and teachers seemed to know when we needed a break. We never had any hint as to when such a free day would come but such days seemed to come at just the right time. We only knew it when the Director would announce it at breakfast, all routines of the day were off. The day was ours for fun, games, ice cream, soda, hikes and sports. These rare days were first class rejuvenators.

We also got home for a month's vacation in August. The freedom of a month's vacation at home was also a test of vocational commitment. I remember undermining my religious commitment on two occasions: once, when I tried to enlist in the Marine Corps at seventeen; the other when I kissed an old girlfriend from grammar school days. The Marine Corps didn't work out because I was seventeen and my parents refused their consent. As for the girlfriend, I bumped into her at a friend's birthday party and felt stirrings I was supposed to avoid or resist. I always managed to return to Ammendale but wondered if my parents ever thought that Aunt Anna was right.

There were also times when I even had doubts about God's existence. I recall expressing my doubts to Brother Henry.

"Brother Henry, is it possible that someone is going to tell me in a couple years that this is all a game; that there is no God and our job is to perpetuate the myth?"

Brother Henry would smile quizzically and shoo me into the chapel. It was too preposterous to warrant a response. Not long after I posed that question I received the shocking news that Brother Daniel, my sponsor, had left the order. He married a girl who worked in the Brothers' refectory at La Salle High. Brother Michael, the school's financial chief, called me into his office to break the news. He knew it could be unsettling but wanted me to hold on. I told him it wouldn't shake my commitment but it did. Not long after I would pack my suitcase and walk down that long, tree lined road. I was going home. But midway down the road, I had a change of heart and returned. to complete my senior year and the senior novitiate.

The Senior Novitiate

After completing high school, the next big step was spending a solid year in a near monastic environment. This year came on the heels of two and a half years spent in a rigorous academic and religious environment at an impressionable age. Now I would undergo an intense year of prayer and meditation. My 19th year was a blur.

The senior novitiate meant moving from our smaller building into the "Big House" or Mother House. It meant the taking of the religious habit, a religious name and a one year vow of poverty, chastity and obedience. It was a year of intense prayer, religious reading, meditation and silence. My religious name was Brother Gerald Robert. I now wore a black robe, a white clerical-style collar such as those worn by European clerics in the 17th century and a black skull cap. Brother Erminus Joseph, the novitiate director, was a living example of the saints whose lives we studied. He exuded both leadership and uncommon serenity. His role was crucial in developing the spiritual character of those who would soon be leading the educational mission of the Order. Like Marine Corps Drill Instructors, the Novitiate Director and his assistants would be responsible for shaping the future force of religious educators.

When my parents visited me in the Junior Novitiate, I was dressed like any regular high school student. But now I was able to greet them in my religious habit. I think this gave my parents the feeling that I was really going through with it. Although I would spend my 19th year going through the motions, the religious life was beginning to lose its grip.

Life became a bit more stimulating once the senior novitiate days were over and college studies began. Normally, college studies were undertaken at a facility in Washington D.C. called the Scholasticate. But our class was diverted from the DC area to a new residence in Elkins Park, Pennsylvania. We took residence in an impressive mansion formerly owned by a prominent family in Elkins Park. The facility was just a few miles from La Salle College, my old high school and my home.

The Elkins Park facilities were easily converted for use as living quarters, classrooms and religious services. For our sleeping quarters, we used rooms formerly used by servants and guests. This was the first time I had a room of my own, small as it was. Everything about the Elkins Park estate reflected beauty and wealth. There were cedar closets not just chests. When I was a kid, a cedar chest provided storage for prized clothing. At Elkins Park, entire rooms were built of cedar. The French windows added to the charm as did the meticulously landscaped grounds. Between the French windows and the manicured grounds, I felt I was living in a castle.

My college curriculum now included US History, physics and philosophy, Spanish, French, Latin and Religion. I did fine in the languages and other courses except for religion. You would expect religious studies to be a slam-dunk for a religious. I can't explain it. I think a personal internal revolt was in progress.

One of my chores at the new location was operating the laundry room in the basement. I ran the washing, drying and ironing operations. I also had a radio. This was the first time in a long time that I had a regular source of information about what was going on in the world. But listening to the radio might have diverted my attention from the gas dryers resulting in the scorching of the Brother Director's new silk pajamas. Nothing was ever said of the incident. Maybe it had something to do with embarrassment on both sides – my mistake and the luxury of silk pajamas for someone with a vow of poverty.

Chapter 3

THE *FIFTIES*

The fifties were dominated by a war in Korea, the McCarthy era of Un-American Activity hearings, Edward R. Murrow's courageous denunciation of McCarthy's tactics, Dwight Eisenhower interstate highway system, the Korean Truce, Khrushchev's shoe banging at the UN, Gary Powers' spy plane incident, Sputnik and a US-Soviet race for missile and space superiority.

Brotherhood Departure

As the radio accounts of Marine exploits at Inchon and the breakout from the Chosen Reservoir unfolded, I began having doubts about my suitability for the religious life. I was feeling confined and restricted, smothered and discontent. I was not happy and wanted to break out of my environment. I wanted to join the Marines.

Earlier, I had discussed these feelings of discontent with Brother Benilde, the director of the Scholasticate. He had recently completed a year of study and spiritual renewal at the Vatican. This exercise was known as the Second Novitiate and often served as a primer for higher and more responsible assignments. As the Director of our scholasticate, he would meet periodically with each Brother to discuss their academic and spiritual progress or any personal concerns. The process gave the Director a unique insight to each Brother's progress and problems. It came to a head in the late spring of my college sophomore year. After months of agonizing over my suitability for the religious life, I concluded the religious life was not for me. It was an amicable departure. I was home the same day I left. But within a year or so I would be back to visit my former associates at Elkins Park. This time I would be wearing the uniform of a Marine sergeant.

Parris Island

Less than two weeks after leaving the Brothers and returning home, I joined the Marine Corps. I don't know what Mom and Dad thought. One minute I was a Brother, the next a Marine. At least I had a job and wouldn't be a financial burden. Besides, I wanted to be a Marine before I wanted to be a Brother.

A lot happens in 12 weeks of training at a Marine Boot camp as anyone who has gone through that experience knows full well. Here was another transformational experience for me as indelible as the religious life experience. About twenty of us soon-to-be Marines left Philadelphia on a train heading for South Carolina. Our destination was the Marine Recruit Training facility at Parris Island. We really didn't know what to expect. But it was an experience none of us would ever forget.

Nothing could have been better to jolt me out of my sheltered existence of the past 5 years than a Marine Boot Camp. It was a sudden awakening to a different world and a nation at war. Many Drill Instructors were wearing the blue and white service ribbon with combat stars that designated in Korea. As often as I fantasized about service in the Marines during WWII, now I was actually part of that organization. I was constantly reminded that I was government property and being trained to be a member of America's most elite fighting force. The Drill Instructors were relentless in their demands and expectations. Recruit treatment was harsher then than it is today. Training practices in the the fifties that resulted in recruit fatalities have since been tempered considerably.

My college experience channeled me into lead and administrative assignments starting with the Philadelphia Recruiting office where I was put in charge of the contingent heading for Parris Island.

"Hey, college boy, you're in charge. Make sure you give these papers to the Platoon Sergeant when you get to Parris Island"

When we got off the train in Beaufort, South Carolina, we immediately boarded a Marine bus. A few minutes later we were on Parris Island and lining up outside a quartermaster building. It was June and it was hot and muggy. Three ramrod straight Drill Instructors in form fitting khaki were there to greet us.

"I am Staff Sergeant Goldsmith. For the next 12 weeks we will be your Drill Instructors and try to make Marines out of you sorry asses. Right now, you're going to trade in your civvies for Marine gear. Soon as you are outfitted, come back here. Form a single line and follow Corporal Strang to the Quartermaster."

These were the gentlest words we would hear over the next 12 weeks. It was a long first day and we were tired. After getting our new Marine gear, we were double timed to a squad bay and up the ladder to the second floor. Lights would be doused in 10 minutes.

The next day began at 5:30AM.

"Alright, you fucking people, rise and shine. You've got fifteen minutes to make your rack, wash, shave and line up outside !"

With these cheery words, the day began. We were shouted at, insulted and literally had our toes stepped on. But we soon learned how to line up and space ourselves.

"Dress right, dress! Looks ragged. Let's try it again!! We would practice the move until Sergeant Goldsmith was satisfied. Then we would march to the mess hall.

"Left, left, left, right, left. Your other left, you fucking idiot!!!" The DI was getting into somebody's face. Not a pleasant encounter. You sought anonymity. You wished you were invisible. If you were out of step, beware. Hardly anyone escaped the personal attention and wrath of a DI.

After marching to the mess hall, we would take a metal tray and metal drinking cup, knife, fork and spoon, pass through the chow line and proceed to mess tables. We stood there until told to sit.

"Ready, seats!!! And hurry up, shit birds. You've got 10 minutes to eat and line-up outside!!!"

Some of the breakfast food was tasty. SOS (shit on a shingle) was real popular. It was creamed hamburger over toast.

Around the late fifties, a record album called "Sounds of Parris Island" came out. You can hear the actual voice commands of drill instructors as they lead recruits through their training. Whether or not you ever experienced Marine recruit training, that record will give you a good idea of the sounds recruits experience daily at Parris Island.

After the first day's breakfast, we were sheared. It took less than 30 seconds and was a great leveling experience. The following twelve weeks of close order drill, physical conditioning, weapons training, studies of Marine history, memorizing general orders, cleaning barracks, cleaning rifles, taking aptitude tests, shining shoes, polishing buckles, washing clothes, being inspected, more close order drill, more barracks cleaning, rifle cleaning, mail calls, mess hall rituals, medical checks, dental checks, fire watches and, if not drilling, doing most things on the double.

Not meeting DI expectations meant countless push-ups, re-cleaning barracks, standing with a 9.5 pound M1 outstretched until somebody dropped. Standing motionless in the sun with an outstretched M1 as sand fleas buzzed about your ears was a real test of self-discipline. This was followed with more close order drill, more classes, more chin ups, push-ups, rope climbs and wall climbs. We were shedding pounds where needed and gaining muscle where it counted. Our physical endurance and self-discipline were improving. But the days seemed too long and the nights too short.

My years in a highly structured religious life were a good primer for the discipline of the military life. My biggest problem was getting used to the four letter words and the tone of voice. With all the prayers and

"Live Jesus in our Hearts" of the past five years, it took awhile to get used to the language and to put more "oomph" into my own voice. But it really snapped me out of the insularity of the religious life. The culture shock was like a splash of cold water.

After weeks of marching countless miles on the grinder, we were getting close to graduation. We were now a long way from our civilian deportment when we enlisted. We were now a disciplined military unit. At graduation we marched to the base band, our left heel hitting the ground in synch with the drumbeat. We had come to enjoy our precision marching especially if the DI had the voice and talent for calling cadence. Only a few were really good at it. Staff Sergeant Goldsmith was one of them. But he could also put the fear of God in you. In one line-up for rifle inspection, Sergeant Goldsmith asked the recruit his name and serial number. The recruit was so flustered he responded by giving the Drill Sergeant's name.

"Sir, my name is Sergeant Goldsmith, sir." I had all I could do to suppress a laugh as did others. Sergeant Goldsmith had a few choice words for the recruit as he threw the recruit's rifle back at him. It was not likely that recruit ever made the same mistake again.

After graduation, we were given a ten day leave along with orders to our next duty station. I was ordered to Camp Pendleton, California. My two years of college slotted me into an administrative occupational specialty. During the leave that followed, I reconnected with my sweetheart from high school days, Bernice Hennessey.

Camp Pendleton

Camp Pendleton is one of the largest military training bases in the country. Established in 1942 with FDR present for its dedication, this sprawling, 305 square mile base has been the primary training site for the Marine Corps, home of the First Marine Division and a staging area for numerous Marine expeditions. Its mountainous terrain and Pacific Ocean frontage makes it ideal for land and amphibious training. I would spend two years of my enlistment assigned to a Headquarters and Service Company prior to being commissioned.

Replacement Drafts

At Pendleton my initial duties involved processing replacements for Marines returning from Korea. Marines getting ready to ship overseas had a checklist of items to complete ranging from immunization shots to powers-of-attorney, and last will and testaments. It also included processing requests for hardship discharges. Most of the hardship cases involved a Marine's family that had fallen on hard times. If the Marine was an only son, he could request a discharge to help his parents. Usually farming or rural families were involved. I remember one case where an eighteen wheeler had plowed through the family home and the Marine in question was an only son. There was even an accompanying photo. I never knew the final disposition of these cases but the experience taught me not to feel sorry for myself. My boss, Tech Sgt Aldrich, was sure I got through mountains of paperwork no matter the hour or how much was involved.

One unexpected surprise in my replacement processing duties was meeting my cousin Vince Finn. Vinny was in a rifle platoon and had about two weeks left at Camp Pendleton before shipping out to Korea. We were able to get together and hoist a few beers on base and in town. We also took a trip to Tijuana for a Thanksgiving dinner at a Chinese restaurant. We both agreed that better Thanksgiving Day dinners were had at home in the States. After Vinny completed his Korean tour in, he returned to civilian life and joined the Philadelphia Fire Department. Two years later, Korea would be the site of another family reunion. This time is would be my brother. Joe was in the Army's special services and his most recent assignment took him to Korea. When I found out where he was located, I managed to get a jeep and visit him. It was like a family reunion.

Legal Office

My next assignment was the Legal Office. My bosses were Captain Victor Salvo and staff sergeant Don Booth. Captain Salvo was a personable officer and a family man. Don was a by-the-book Marine and member of the Marine Rifle Team. Years later, Don would obtain a Ph.D and become a Political Science professor at Chapman College in Orange,

California. Our legal office handled courts-martial and investigations. My court recording responsibilities resulted in stenographic schooling at the nearby Point Loma Naval training center. This wasn't the kind of duty a Marine would normally request but it provided a change of pace and scenery for a few weeks. The demand on my stenographic skills were, however, meager. I soon lost whatever skill I had and resorted to using a steno-mask. Meanwhile, I was moving up in the ranks. I was now a sergeant.

One of the investigations our legal office conducted involved a hit-and-run death of a Marine hiking on Highway 101. In preparing the return of the Marine's personal effects to his wife on the east coast, we came upon some letters and photos indicating an affair with a west coast girl. These were excluded from the returned personal effects. I considered this discretion a compliment to the sensibility of the staff handling the matter.

Naval Training Center

With orders in hand to attend the Steno School at Point Loma, I joined a class of about twenty Marines all assigned to the Steno School. We were being taught the Gregg Simplified shorthand method, a manual technique popular at the time. Chief Gibbs and his assistant were excellent instructors. I must admit that while at the school I did develop a passable skill in shorthand. But infrequent use after my return to Pendleton put those skills in the rusty column. So I resorted to use of a stenomask. This mask covered the nose and mouth so you could repeat what was being said without disturbing others. What I repeated into the mask was recorded and later transcribed. It worked to the satisfaction of the court, the prosecution and the defense.

While at the Naval Training Center, you still couldn't get the Marine out of us even while attending an administrative school. The Naval Training Center, in addition to its many technical schools, was home to the Navy's west coast Recruit Training Center. People marched everywhere - from classes to mess halls. We pitted our marching proficiency against the Navy's and took the prize hands down. Years later, I would be witness the closing of the Naval Training Center.

All activities would be transferred to the Navy's Great Lakes Center. The Point Loma site would be transformed into a private housing, commercial and educational complex.

Off-Duty Activities

My religious beliefs were still strong in those days. I volunteered my services to the Catholic base chaplain, Father Cornelius Griffin, a Navy Commander. Father Connie had part of his jaw shot off in Korea while administering the last rites to severely wounded Marines in the thick of battle. He was awarded the Navy Cross for his bravery. His sermons at Sunday mass were always inspiring and conversations with him were never dull. He enjoyed bourbon and water and could hold his own with the best. Another of his volunteers included Bill Gay, a former Trappist monk, who would go on to become a Marine fighter pilot.

I found the opportunities for continuous learning and keeping in shape almost limitless. I enrolled in correspondence courses offered by the Marine Corps Institute, attended Spanish classes at Oceanside Community College and routinely hitched to San Diego to use the YMCA pool.

Hitching a ride in California in the early fifties was easy to do, especially if you were in uniform. But it came with its share of risks. In those days, it wasn't unusual to be picked by someone who was drinking. I don't know how many times I was offered a drink as we sped down 101. It was doubly exciting given California's three lane highway system. The center lane was up for grabs in either direction. When you opted to move ahead of a slower vehicle, you had to make sure you could move fast enough to avoid a collision with a car coming from the opposite direction. Sometimes it felt like a continuous game of chicken or Russian roulette.

Tijuana

Tijuana was a popular watering hole for Marines. We usually went there as a group and most often in civilian clothes. We were also fortunate enough to have a car lent to us by a trusting Private Benjamin who only wanted his car back in one piece with a full tank of gas. When we finished navigating the three lane highway to the border, we would be waved across the border with only one question from the Mexican border guard – "what is the purpose of your visit, business or pleasure?"

Avenida Revoluccion was loaded with bars, girlie shows and opportunities for getting laid. It was here that, after many sexless years as a religious, I had my first introduction to sex. It was fast and not very satisfying. I think it cost me five dollars. I didn't think it was worth it and couldn't wash myself off fast enough. I had visions of catching VD. All those WWII venereal disease training films flashed through my mind including those graphic photos of diseased sex organs. My Marine buddies, however, didn't seem to have any such qualms.

Within our small band there was one Marine the girls called 'superman'. The girls vied for his attention praising his endowment and stamina. Although the other Marines might have felt a tinge of envy, "superman's draw power expanded the bevvy of women to choose from.

On one of my last trip's to Tijuana, the engine blew about midway back to the base We had to leave the car alongside the road in Encinitas and hitch back to the base. When we returned a few days later in a tow truck, the car was gone. We never found it. We still owe Private Benjamin about a hundred bucks for his car.

Bernie, Barracks Life and OCS

About this time, I took a short leave and returned to Philadelphia. Besides spending some time with family and friends, my major objective was to persuade Bernie to come out to California so we could spend some time together. A short time after I returned to Pendleton, Bernie joined me and spent a week at the guest lodging right on the base. I was working at the Replacement Draft center at the time but managed to get a couple days leave. We rented a car, took in the San Diego sights and even made a trip to Mexico's Rosarita Beach. On the way back, we stopped at a motel near the Mexican border. Bernie slept in the bed and I slept on a couch. At the time, a popular tune called Blue Tango seemed to follow us wherever we went. Even thinking back on that time, that tune comes to mind. When I returned to Pendleton, Tech Sergeant Aldrich, noticed my starry-eyed condition and had some words of advice.

"Byron, for Christ's sake, you better get it on."

Aldrich was married and lived off base. Always blunt with his advice, he continued:

"One thing about marriage is that you can satisfy your amorous moods whenever you want."

Those were not his exact words. He put it in more graphic Marine language. Bernie returned to Philadelphia and her job as a dental hygienist. My amorous moods would be put on hold for another year.

Barracks Life

My life at Camp Pendleton was spent in two different living environments. One was in two story wooden barracks located at the central command or main headquarters area. The other was spent in a tent and Quonset hut at remote camp sites located several miles north of the main base and several miles inland from the ocean and Pacific Highway. One was called Las Pulgas (the fleas) or Tent Camp I; the other was called San Onofre or Tent Camp II. San Onofre was just a few miles south of San Clemente, a small, attractive town on the sourthernmost edge of Orange County. Bernie and I would spent our last months together in a small apartment prior to shipping overseas.

While the Korean War was in progress, the Marine Corps was accepting draftees. Some of these draftees were married and often the butt of teasing.

"Hey, if the Marine Corps wanted you to have a wife they would have issued you one."

Some of the married draftees who lived off base would retort by recounting the joys of married life. But early morning barracks' banter preceeding a march to the mess hall was often overshadowed by the blare of a radio. One popular radio advertisement at the time was a recruiting jingle used by San Diego's largest aircraft manufacturer. General Dynamics Convair was one of San Diego's largest employers. At its height during WWII it employed some 40,000 workers making B-24 Liberator bombers and PBY 5's. Now it was making the nation's first delta winged jet fighter, the F102. Job opportunities were being announced over the barrack's radio every morning with a catchy jingle.

"Let's all get a job at Convair; we'll make more money there!"

Every time that jingle played, about half the squad bay would join in. A lot of Marines would end up working for Convair if they remained in San Diego when they got out. I was one of them.

We also had occasional skirmishes among ourselves that were settled out behind the barracks. For some forgotten reason, I had a settlement issue that left a fellow Marine with a black eye and bloody nose. But we were reminded of worse fates when the Officer-of-the-Day would read court martial punishments to Marines lined up for chow. Punishments usually included brig time, reduction in rank, fines and, in many instances, a less than honorable discharge. These were sobering reminders to hungry Marines that the Corps was dead serious about its discipline requirements.

Discipline is at the core of Marine success. But the Corps is also sensitive to the needs of its Marines. Duty officers would often ask Marines for suggestions on how to improve conditions. It wouldn't be long before I would be in a position to do likewise.

Night life in the barracks had its share of fun and annoyances. One common annoyance was being awakened by a slightly inebriated Marine returning from liberty after lights were out. You would be sleeping when a hand would shake your shoulder waking you up and asking with beery breath:

"Are you asleep? Just checking."

Nothing is more conducive to retaliation.

Officer Candidate School

Soon after Bernie returned to Philadelphia, I applied for flight school via a Naval Cadet program that accepted enlisted men who met the qualifications. But my poor depth perception disqualified me. I then decided to apply for Officer Candidate School. With recommendations from my company commander, First Lieutenant Wendell O. Beard, Legal Office chief, Captain Victor Salvo and the Replacement Draft commander, Lieutenant Buckley, I was off to Quantico, Virginia.

The Officer Candidate School (OCS) was ten weeks of the most grueling weeks of my life. When you went to OCS, you were stripped of all rank. You wore an OC (Officer Candidate) pin on your collar and that was it. You were physically exercised to a near breaking point and psychologically evaluated to assess how well you performed under stress. Your leadership and teamwork skills were tested as were your creativity problem solving skills. Your peers also got to rate you by responding to questions like "would you want so-and-so to be with you in a combat situation?"

As usual with the Marines, there was a lot of running and endurance testing. These helped determine individual tenacity, drive and a never-give-up attitude. Although on endurance runs I would usually end up in the first three or four, it was a result of my running additional miles outside the regular training regimen.

One of the more stressful exercises used to test your presence of mind was when two officers were pitted against you, each asking a different question at the same time, one in front of you, the other behind you; one tapping you on the head, the other asking how you would handle a Marine disobeying an order in combat. All the while, each officer was telling you to ignore the other. There were also batteries of aptitude, intelligence and psychological profile tests.

There were class times when physical fatigue and the warm Virginia weather were conducive to nodding off during a lecture. But the course leaders had a remedy for that – a Mark 2 flash banger. When heads would nod, a grenade-like Mark 2 would roll down the aisle near anyone nodding off. The Mark 2 explodes with an ear shattering bang. That always brought everyone back to an alert status for the remainder of the class.

When the vetting process of this screening course ended, there came the "moment of truth". On the final day we were ordered to leave our barracks and line-up our front. A truck and a pile of seabags were nearby. Names were called. Those called were directed to pick up their seabags and get on the truck. Those of us who remained were congratulated. We were now officers in the United States Marine Corps - second lieutenants with permanent reserve commissions, gentlemen by an act of Congress. A uniform ceremony and the pinning of gold bars would take place later that day followed by a ten day leave. Afterwards, we would report back to Quantico for six months of Basic School training.

I'm not sure how I managed to get married in the short a time between completing OCS and reporting to the 23rd SBC, Special Basic Class, at Quantico. It was 1953 and the Korean War was still in progress. Little did we know the Korean truce would be signed before our graduation.

Bernie and I were married at St. Vincent's Catholic Church in Mt Airy, a Philadelphia suburb that bordered Germantown. Father Dougherty, a relative on Grandpa Finn's side, performed the ceremony. My parents, brother Joe, Bernice's parents, aunts, uncles and cousins Jack and Bobbie O'Donnell, both of whom would soon join the Air Force, Bill Merkel a boyhood friend and even the director of my junior novice days at Ammendale, Brother Henry. We left the church in a shower of rice, enjoyed a reception and drove off to a hotel in Washington DC. After a wedding night in DC, we proceeded to our new residence in Fredericksburg, Virginia.

Fredericksburg is a classic southern city. Its founding goes back to 1728. George Washington's mother and James Monroe both lived there for awhile. It was also the scene of a Confederate victory in the early phase of the Civil War. Robert E. Lee turned back an attack on Virginia by Union General Burnside in 1862. There were bullet holes from that campaign still visible in some of the wooden shutters on older structures. There was also the anomaly of racial segregation. The train stations still had restrooms and drinking fountains marked "Coloreds Only." We occupied the second floor of a spacious home on Hanover Street. Nancy Waller Payne, our landlady, was as gracious as any lady you could imagine from the old South. She introduced us to mint juleps.

Special Basic School

Basic school was another period of intense of learning but without the pressure of Boot Camp or Officer Candidate School. We were introduced to the whole arsenal of Marine weapons and basic tactics. We experienced the overhead swoosh of artillery and the hiss of a flame thrower's bleeder valve. Sometimes there was the surprise of someone forgetting to clear his rifle followed by a discharge when the trigger was pulled.

There were night exercises and coming home in the wee morning hours with M1 slung over the shoulder. We were expected to be back on base and ready for inspection at the regular time. Many wives including mine helped us prepare for inspections by cleaning our rifles and taking a blitz cloth to our belt buckles. Some wives also packed lunches for their men. Bernie packed mine and I gained weight.

About the second month into our training, the Korean truce was declared. This was welcome news for everyone especially the wives. It did not affect the training, however, which continued at the same rigorous pace.

Bernie was in her second month of pregnancy when we left Quantico, bid farewell to Fredericksburg and drove across the country in a 49 Plymouth to Camp Pendleton. We took an apartment in San Clemente, a charming coastal town just a few miles north the Pendleton Tent Camp where I was to report. Schooling, physical conditioning, and getting all the necessary shots would take place over the next couple weeks in preparation for going overseas. Now I was part of the real Marine Corps, the FMF (Fleet Marine Force). Gone were the administrative duties of my enlisted days.

Tent Camp and Overseas

My Tent Camp Commanding Officer was a First Lieutenant Frank V. Cutting, a long time Marine and mustang officer. He was a legend in the surrounding communities and known for riding his horse into a local bar and ordering a drink. I remember being in his tent when a young Marine was called in for a dressing down on some issue. He said something that angered Cutting and before I knew it an object was sailing towards a Marine's head. Luckily, it missed.

One of the duties I didn't particularly like was being the company paymaster. At that time we were paid in cash monthly. You had to count and sign out for a cash payroll for the entire company. The cash was in new bills which meant you had to be careful counting it out. If you came up short, it came out of your pocket. One times I did come up short. I was out twenty dollars.

Just before my scheduled overseas departure, I was granted leave to get Bernie back home to Philadelphia. I wanted Bernie's mother and my parents to look after her while I was gone. We made the drive back to Philadelphia in 72 hours but my leave time was so short I had to turn around almost immediately and fly back.

It wasn't long before we were aboard a troop ship, APA Okanagan, and saying goodbye to San Diego. Seasickness was the next challenge. This is one of life's most debilitating experiences. Ask any Marine prone to seasickness about his first experience at sea on a troop carrier. It means heaving, buckets, mops, no eating, weakness and more heaving. Dying becomes a welcome thought. But after 4 or 5 days, your system adjusts to the ship's motion. You can eat again and the heaves are just a bad memory.

Japan

It took about 3 weeks to get to Yokosuka, Japan from San Diego because we played war games on the way. For city boys, being afloat that long makes you a real believer in the amount of water that covers this planet. You could almost be convinced that land no longer existed.

Once seasickness is over, life at sea isn't that bad especially if you are an officer. At meal time, Filipino stewards served as waiters and cooks. You ate off white plates trimmed with blue anchors. There were clean white table cloths and cloth napkins. Our sleeping quarters were cabin spaces on the upper levels as opposed to stacked bunks at the lower levels. This was an unaccustomed luxury for me. On land, however, unless you were at a permanent installation, it was a different story. When it came to living in the field, all Marines, officer and enlisted alike, roughed it and shared a life of bare essentials.

Getting off a boat after almost a month at sea is an experience. The ground seemed to be rolling. It reminded me of some of the great rolls at sea we experienced. On occasion, the ship listed to the side so steeply, I would have taken bets we were going over. But within a few minutes back on land, my internal gyroscope stabilized and the earth felt steady. The feel of steady land felt good.

Yokosuka is a bustling port city where cars and bicycles seemed to move in every direction at once. We were given a couple hours to stretch our legs and I got my first glance at Japan's traffic protocols. Just a few feet in front of me, a car knocked a cyclist off his bike. The biker got up, brushed himself off, than bowed apologetically to the driver of the car. I thought the action should have been reversed. But both went their way and that was that. Soon after we retrieved our gear and were trucked out to Middle Camp Fuji.

Middle Camp Fuji is located next to a small town called Gotemba and at the base of Japan's sacred mountain, Mount Fujiyama. This 12,388 foot high volcanic mountain with its snowy peak dominated the landscape. It is a major attraction for tourists and hikers. I would wake up to this majestic sight daily while in camp. I was assigned to a Weapons Company. Our training schedule would soon put us back aboard ships and to field maneuvers at sites that were once the scene of WWII's bloodiest Pacific battles.

A Weapons Company is designed to increase the lethality of a Marine rifle company. Components of a Weapons Company can vary but mine included machine guns, mortars and anti-tank weapons. I was in charge of both water and air-cooled, 30 calibre machine guns. I re-familiarized myself with those weapons, taking them apart, cleaning, re-assembling, test firing and reviewing deployment strategies. Thanks to my platoon sergeant my re-familiarization was completed in short order. Other elements included 81 millimeter mortars and anti-tank rocket launchers. These elements were attached to Rifle Companies during field operations. I took pride in having my machine gunners reach their objectives even before the riflemen who had less to carry.

Newly minted Marine second lieutenant 1953

Bernice Hennessey, bride to be 1953

The newly weds 1953

On maneuvers. Okinawa. 1954

Linking up with brother Joe in Korea 1954

Typical village scene in Korea 1954.

Life at Middle Camp Fuji was comfortable. We took our meals in a nicely appointed dining room tended by a hired staff of Japanese. We also had an Officers Club. The sign above the club door read "He Who Wears His Hat in Here Must Buy the House a Round of Cheer". The message must have really gotten across. I never remember anyone ordering drinks for the house.

Our uniforms were cleaned and pressed and our utilities washed and neatly folded by Japanese maids who probably enjoyed one of the better paying jobs in the area. Our shoes were also shined and beds made. As members of the 3rd battalion, 5th Marines we were entitled to wear the fourragere, a braided cord worn over the left shoulder with a whistle-like pendant on the end. This commemorated an award made by the French to the Marines for valor during WWI. Anyone serving in the 3rd battalion, 5thMarines was entitled to wear the award as long as they were attached to the unit. It was also a time when the swagger stick was in vogue and Marine officers would carry them. This baton-like stick was an authority symbol about 24 inches long. But its usage varied over time depending on the preference of a base commander or the Commandant.

Those of us who served during the Korean era time did not have much to show in terms of ribbons. For career Marines, however, their ribbons tell their career history. I often thought a ribbon display might also have a place in the civilian world. Ribbons could reflect civilian participation in different classes of industry or community services such as defense, local-state-federal government, school systems and other categories.

One of the Japanese girls who serviced our section of the BOQ was Yoshiko. She was young but old enough to remember the bombings during the war, especially the incendiary bombs that played havoc with the wooden structures of Japanese housing. She would tell us about her experience and the terror caused by the incendiary bombs. "Takson bakadon" she would say - many bombs.

Yoshko also used our shower facilities now and then. If her timing was off, we would find Yoshko naked as a jaybird as we entered the shower. But there would be little embarrassment. Nudity is taken as a matter of course in Japan. Both sexes bathe together communally all the time, a custom popularized by Japan's many hot bath houses. We are the ones who have a hang-up with nudity.

Many military personnel also take advantage of Hong Kong's famous tailoring community. You select the material and cut, have your measurements taken and within a couple of weeks you have an inexpensive, well-tailored suit. One evening, several of us decided to go to town in our new suits It was night and we were walking three abreast down dirt road enroute to the local train station. John Daley, a fellow lieutenant from my home town of Philadelphia and graduate of the Jesuit-run St. Joseph's College, suddenly disappeared. I looked over at Bob Moynihan, another lieutentant from New York who bore the moniker "Mad Dog" and then we both looked down. John emerged from the deepest pothole I ever saw. What was worse, the pothole was filled with water. John's new suit, white when he fell in, was now black. A Japanese gardener who was watering plants nearby and witnessed the scene bellowed with laughter. This infuriated John who took the hose from the man and watered him. The night's outing was scrubbed. We returned to the base and capped the evening with a few drinks at the Officers' Club.

Generally, times off the base where interesting and pleasant experiences. But there were still some restaurant-bar locations where resentment of the American presence lingered. It didn't take long to get the message when service was not forthcoming. But I recall an encounter where I was to blame. One such instance involved a hotel in Kyoto where I had spent the night. When I was about to leave I was unable to find my money. I reported this to the hotel manager. He lined up the entire staff and questioned them regarding the missing money. The outcome was negative. On the train back to Middle Camp Fuji I discovered the missing money. It was caught in my trouser waistband. How it got there I'll never know. But I felt embarrassed that I had mistakenly put a cloak of suspicion over the hotel staff. The Japanese have a reputation for honesty. This is a nation that at that time most did not even bother to lock their doors.

Okinawa

Okinawa was our first site to train for an amphibious exercise and land maneuver in mountainous terrain. On the way to these island war games, three of us, all lieutenants, were called into the commanding officer's cabin and ordered to standby for a potential airlift into Dienbienphu. It was April 1954. The French were in the throes of seeing its Far East colonial empire collapse. Dienbienphu was one of the last French outposts and it was surrounded by Vietnamese. The French were taking heavy casualties from the artillery fire pouring down from the surrounding hills plus assaults by a large Vietnamese ground force. We were briefed on the status and told to be ready to helicopter from the ship to the battle site the next day. Our mission was primarily to observe, learn and advise. We were selected because of the foreign language skills noted in our qualification jackets. I was tabbed for French, another Marine for German and another, Dutch. We were told not to say anything to anyone about the mission. The next day, however, we were told to stand down. The mission had been scrubbed. Dienbienphu had capitulated. The French rule in Indochina was over.

From the ship, Okinawa's golden beaches and palm trees looked like a Hollywood movie set. It didn't look real. We were getting used to climbing down rope ladders hanging over the side of the ship into landing craft. Once our landing craft made the beaches, we used our maps to move on to the designated objectives, usually high ground in a mountainous area. We would then live in the field for few days advancing towards our objective and consolidating our positions. One thing I found to be an impediment to effective fighting was the weight of our backpacks. If I had my way, Marines would carry only bare essentials - weapons, ammo and water. Carrying excess weight was tiring and impeded fast movement. I was an advocate of living off the land if at all possible. Standard logistic support could follow. I also favored the rough and tumble of physical contact among my platoon members and had them engage in"king of the hill" type wrestling matches for exercise. As regards shooting skills, something prized by the Marine Corps, I was a strong advocate of more time for practice shooting on the range during off duty hours.

On the last day of our field exercise, an F4U Corsair that was simulating close air support crashed into a mountain side. I watched from a distance as the pilot approached the mountain in a steep dive. I sensed the pilot was not going to be able to pull out of the dive. He slammed into the mountain side and the craft exploded.

After completing our field exercises, we reported to Kadena Air Base. The showers, the mess hall and a swimming pool were a welcome relief.

It was hard to imagine that only nine years ago Okinawa was the scene of the bloodiest battle of the Pacific. The battle began in April and ended 3 months later in June 1945. During that same period, Franklin Roosevelt died, Mussolini was executed, Hitler committed suicide and the Germans surrendered. Two months later in August, the first atomic bomb was dropped on Hiroshima and the Emperor announced Japan's surrender. General MacArthur accepted the formal surrender of Japan aboard the battleship Missouri in early September.

Once back at sea, we headed for Iwo Jima. While on board, we buried the F4U pilot killed when his plane crashed into the mountainside a few days earlier. It was sad to witness a young pilot's shrouded body slide from under a tilted, flag-covered board into the deep.

Iwo Jima

Following Okinawa, we were back at sea once again. This time our maneuvers would take us to Iwo Jima. I was assigned to umpire duties which meant monitoring the performance of designated units as they pursued their maneuver objectives. As an umpire, I had a lot of freedom of movement. I covered most of that 2x5 mile, pork chop-shaped island on foot. I trekked to the top of Mt. Surabachi, scene of the most memorable flag raising event of the war and the nation's most recognizable symbol of Marine valor in WWII. At that time, the American flag flew twenty-four hours a day atop Surabachi.

Every rock on that island was pock-marked by bullets or shell fragments. Casualties were high on both sides. It was Japan's first defense of its own soil. Very few Japanese were taken prisoner. Walking that island, I was surprised to find dead Japanese still in caves with hair on their heads. The sulphur acted as a preservative. Most of the island smelled like sulphur. I found it hard to believe that sugar cane grew there but it did.

At night, stretched out on a sleeping bag on the black sand and looking up at a star-studded Pacific sky, I thought of how different life might have been for me had I been born earlier than I had. But for the accident of a birth date, I might have been in that battle. A friend of mine, retired Sergeant Major Bill Paxton, himself a Marine legend, lost his Marine father on Iwo Jima. I would get to know Bill some fifty years later when I was developing a charter school. Not long after, I would renew my Marine Corps ties by joining the Marine Historical Society at the Marine Recruit Depot in San Diego.

Back in Japan, life at Middle Camp Fuji settled back into a routine. Being able to get off the base occasionally on week-ends let me pursue things Japanese. I bought a language book and began familiarizing myself with Katakana. I began picking up simple but useful phrases like "where does this train go", "where is the bathroom", "hello", goodbye", thank you", "I'm fine" "good day", "good evening", etc. I also picked up the traditional gifts like Mikimoto pearls, a Geisha outfit and a Japanese baby doll.

I enjoyed eating in Japanese restaurants especially their mix of rice, chicken and peas. I liked eating with chopsticks and drinking warm saki. On occasion I would wear a comfortable kimono and native footwear, the wooden geta. One of my favorite stopovers was the resort town of Atami.

I liked the efficiency of the Japanese trains. They really ran on schedule and the train conductors made sure all available space was taken. At their busiest hours, the conductors would pack people into trains like sardines.

I was also impressed by the industriousness of the Japanese. At all hours of the day or night, activity never ceased. I wondered when they slept. I admired the precision of their workmanship especially the carpentry exhibited in their wooden homes, their personal and household cleanliness and the bath ritual. Even removing shoes before entering a dwelling enhanced the cleanliness of their living quarters. It seemed as though every blade of grass in that country was individually cultivated.

I became familiar with Japanese music and dance thanks to the hospitality of the Mama-sans who ran the bordellos. The major attraction of these houses was sex, booze and hot baths. Although I put myself in harms way by visiting these houses, my activities were usually limited to a massage and hot bath. But the musical preliminaries and the folk dances performed by the girls made a lasting impression. I enjoyed the sounds of the stringed samisen, songs like China Night and dances like the Tanko Bushi and Soran Bushi. The dances were performed in a single line with the dancers imitating the motions of the activity described in the song. The Tanko Bushi was the coal miner's dance whose motions mimicked those of a miner shoveling coal. The Soran Bushi was a fisherman'dance with motions suggesting the tossing of a net overboard and hauling the catch onto the deck. The dances were very gracefully performed by the Geisha-like entertainers with the customers invited to participate. I was becoming culturally attuned. This musical experience made a lasting impression. Back home, I would demonstrate the dances to my family and friends. Later, these dances would be included among the repertoire of some of folk dance clubs my family would join.

The luxury of Japan came to an end, however, when many of us were transferred to Korea. It was goodbye Third Marine Division, Middle Camp Fuji with its comfortable billeting and hello to the First Marine Division and a Spartan lifestyle at the 38th parallel. Life as a field Marine resumed. This time I was assigned as a platoon leader in a rifle company.

Korea

South Korea was hot in the summer and cold in the winter. It is known as the "land of the morning calm" because of the stillness associated with its mornings when a low mist hovers over the rice fields. But life in a tent camp didn't have many frills. The fleshpots of Japan were now a memory.

There were the usual field exercises, classes, inspections, sports and conditioning routines. Our primary mission was to serve as the first line of defense at the 38th parallel. We rotated assignments from the trench lines and to our camp. On marches to and from the 38th, we always stayed on a worn path. The danger of unexploded landmines still existed.

At the 38th parallel, we manned trench lines and bunkers about two hundred yards south of the actual 38th parallel. The North Koreans maintained a similar distance gap north of the 38th. On each of my flanks, I had a contingent of United Nation forces - South Korean Marines on one side and Turks on the other. I struck up a friendship with my Turkish counterpart, a Lieutenant Ataturk. We became friends and even exchanged letters after we had both separated from the service. The Turkish troops looked older than our Marines but it may have been the swarthiness of their complexion that gave them an older look. They had a reputation for being fierce fighters especially in close combat. The North Koreans and Chinese feared their bayonets.

I learned something new from my Turkish counterpart, Lietenant Ataturk. It was the sport of camel wrestling. Camel wrestling was the furthest thing from my mind in Korea and I don't remember how the subject up. I remember we were putting our own marksmanship to the test with our side-arms when the topic came up. I had just impressed him with a lucky shot that split a rock some 15-20 yards away. He went on to describe a popular contest in his country involving camels. Two camels would vie with one another in a test of neck strength. The camel that could pin the neck of the other camel to the ground won. Many years later I would come across that sport in a film on Turkey that I was presenting to a class on International Relations and Cultures. Needless to say, it brought back memories of my meeting with Lt. Ataturk on the 38th parallel.

Our job on the 38th parallel was to be the first line of defense in the event of hostilities. I have never felt such a sense of responsibility for the lives of other Marines as I did then. In fact, I am yet to rival that sense of responsibility for the lives of others..

Flowing close to our encampment was the Imjin River. We immortalized that river in song. Almost nightly, we invoked that river's name as we sang about our fantasy of booze being transported to the Officer's club over its waters.

"They say there's a barge on the Imjim, they say it is loaded with beer, they say there's a barge on the Imjim, oh, Lordy when will it get here". This verse was followed by a litany of other alcoholic beverages like whiskey, vodka and beer.

Until I got to Korea, I didn't smoke and even my drinking was very moderate.. But I began to smoke there and my drinking kicked up a notch. But drinking had its practical side in Korea. Except for our own treated water, the Korean was not considered safe for drinking. Any canned or bottled liquid was considered safer than the water. I even brushed my teeth with beer and carried Korean wine in my canteen.

Our camp was situated just outside the small town of Paju-ri. The population at the time could not have been more than a couple thousand. Small vendor stalls lined the main road that cut through the middle of town. On one occasion, I bought some candles for our tent in case our generators went down. You can imagine my surprise when I found that the candles I bought there were made in Philadelphia, my home town..

Our laundry was done by local women and the local boys kept our shoes shined. I marveled at how white the Korean women could get our clothes by washing them by a stream of running water and beating them with sticks. I found the formal attire of mature men strikingly different than the kimonos worn in Japan. The Koreans wore flowing white robes with stovepipe black hats. Sometimes the men sported long beards. They also smoked pipes with stems that were 18 to 20 inches long. Lighting a pipe was a two man operation. The women also wore robes that were more colorful than those worn by men. Although the dress of the Japanese geisha was more intricate and colorful, I found the Korean women more attractive in terms of facial beauty than the Japanese.

To help offset the cold Korean winters and our drafty tent floors, I managed to work a deal with a Korean local for straw floor mats. These mats would reduce the drafts coming up through the tent flooring. As I met the mat dealer at the base entry gate, I got a call from the company CO asking how I paid for the mats. I told him chewing gum. It could have been bad news had I said MPC, the military currency. It was not to be used off base in Korea. Like many civilian reservists recalled to active duty and assigned to infantry outfits to qualify more readily for promotion to field grade, my CO was a lawyer and a stickler for regulations. He even had cards made out for all his officers regarding the Miranda warning that we should use when a Marine was suspected of a punishable offense. So the mats came aboard without incident and tent drafts reduced considerably. However, we still had rats to contend with. At night when the lights were out and almost everyone asleep, you could hear the rats jumping for goodies we suspended from the tent ceiling to keep them out of reach of these pesky infiltrators. We also had other infiltrators – women.

Women from the neighboring village would somehow manage to get through the base fencing and slip into Marine sleeping bags. When I was Officer of the Day, rousting these intruders off the base was part of my job to the disappointment of the Marines. Some of those girls managed to pick up my name and when marching through town on the way to field exercises, some the girls would wave and say "Hi, Lieutenant Bob". It was a little embarrassing.

Marines, however, take pride in contributing to communities near their bases. One of our favorite contributions involves school construction. It was always a pleasure to pass a school built with our help and hear the children singing. A very popular song that could be heard passing almost any school was the Arirang. This is a Korean folk song that is as revered as the Korean national anthem.

The personal generosity of Marines serving abroad helps build friendship and trust. Over the Christmas period, Bernie sent me a number of toys for the Korean kids. In making the village rounds as Santa Claus, I always got the seat of honor which happened to be on the floor directly over a heating pipe that ran underneath. A seat over the heating pipe On cold Korean nights that was a prized seat. As for Korean food, kimchi, a vegetable and garlic-laced mixture, was the national dish and as popular as the Japanese equivalent, sukiyaki. Unless your breath reeked of kimchi, you were considered underfed. I ate it but preferred sukiyaki.

One very pleasant surprise in Korea was meeting up with my brother Joe. Joe was in an Army Special Services unit that was entertaining Army troops in Korea. Joe was a stand-up comic, Hollywood star impersonator, a singer and a musician. What a carryback to the thirties and Bringhurst Street with Mom at the piano, Dad singing and Uncle Mike tap dancing. Joe's talented entourage included the nationally famous accordionist Dick Contino. When I heard Joe was in Korea and stationed not too far from our camp, I managed to get a jeep and drive out to his post. It was an enjoyable reunion at a point on the globe that only American foreign policy could make happen.

In April 1954 I got the word. I was now the proud father of a baby girl. What a feeling. But a year would pass before I would get to see and hold her. I had a lot to look forward to.

About mid- point in our Korean tour we were given a few days of R&R (rest and recuperation) in Japan. It was a treat to return to a developed country with lots of amenities. There was also the humorous Catch 22 of where you caught a venereal disease if you were unfortunate enough to catch it. If you caught the disease while in Japan on R&R, there was no disciplinary action. If you caught it in Korea, there was a presumption that you violated camp restrictions and were subject to disciplinary action. I never saw this played out for real but Marine legal casuists had a lot of fun toying with various scenarios.

Back in Japan, I spent a few days at Atami and Kyoto, took a lot of pictures, sent some souvenirs home and enjoyed the chicken, rice, sukiyaki and hot sake. On the flight back to Korea, the weather was rough and I swear we missed a mountain top by inches. Upon landing, I sought out a Catholic chaplain and had my confession heard. I had strayed from the straight and narrow while on R&R and the near brush with death was a wake-up call to put my spiritual affairs in order. I was still on good terms with the Catholic Church and I wanted it to stay that way. My split with the church was still a couple years away.

Back in Korea, I found myself assigned as a defense attorney for a Marine being court-martialed. I forget the charge but I remember taps being played as I made my concluding remarks. Although the evidence against my client was irrefutable, the drama of the concluding remarks together with taps playing in the background may have lessened the penalty. On another occasion, I enjoyed the satisfaction of having the veil of suspicion lifted from one of my platoon members when the accuser failed to identify the offender from a line-up I arranged.

Return to San Diego

With the birth of my daughter, the months went by slowly. But departure day finally arrived. We packed our gear, boarded a ship and headed back to San Diego. This time there was no seasickness. I had sea legs now. I took leave immediately upon my return and had a joyful reunion in Philadelphia with Bernie, baby Ginny, Mom and Dad.

After a few days of re-acquaintance with family, friends and neighbors, it was time to head back for my discharge and the start of a new life in San Diego. I would be repeating an exodus from Philadelphia that many other servicemen made after WWII. I had fallen in love with San Diego's climate and cleanliness ever since I was first assigned to Camp Pendleton. Now I was returning and setting my sights on completing college and beginning a new life with a new wife and a new baby.

With the help of some military friends we found a small apartment not far from downtown San Diego and just across the street from a Catholic church. I wasted no time enrolling for the summer session at San Diego State, applying for the GI education assist, signing up for the college veteran housing and getting a part time job as a cab driver and city lifeguard. I was given credit for my previous college work and military experience and would be able to satisfy requirements for a bachelor's degree with a summer session and a full course load in the fall and spring. I chose a general major: Political Science, US History and French. Then I took a full time night job as a parcel loader for

United Parcel. The job paid well and the Teamster benefits were great. About the only time I had to sleep was on weekends but my grades were excellent. I made the Dean's list and received an achievement award for Political Science.

At the time, the Communist scare was dominating the news. Senator Joe McCarthy's Un-American Activity Committee hearings were making the news particularly his accusations directed towards the Hollywood set. Edward R. Murrow was one of the few leaders who had the guts to stand up to him. I remember writing an article at the time entitled "But He Doesn't Eat Wheaties, Joe", a satire on McCarthy's attempt to smear citizens on the slightest pretext.

With the United Parcel job, the GI bill and the low rent college housing at the Aztec Terrace, we were making it. The housing location was excellent. It was close to Presidio Park where Bernie could take Ginny for strolls during the day, close to San Diego's historic Old Town and close to a manufacturing and procurement site of San Diego's largest defense contractor, General Dynamics.

Bernie was pregnant again. This time it was a boy. Mark was born in April but it wasn't an easy birth. His umbilical cord had wrapped from around his neck during birth giving us all a scare. But Mark made it. I was a proud father again.

After graduation I applied for graduate school and was accepted into the master's program for Public Administration. Meantime, I took a full time day job at the nearby Convair plant as an hourly worker assisting a salaried buyer. A few months later, I was promoted to salaried buyer.

The Convair plant was in easy walking distance to our apartment in the Aztec Terrace. Since I was carrying a full graduate course load at night, I was still eligible for GI benefits and college housing. Some great friendships were made during our days at the Aztec Terrace. The former GIs were serious students. On campus, we were known as the damn average raisers. We were more interested in learning than partying. One of my mathematician friends, Frank Chadwick, who worked for the new Astronautics Division of General Dynamics, got me interested in his scuba diving sport. On many an early Saturday or Sunday morning we could be found underwater at the La Jolla Cove prying abalone from the rocks with tire irons and enjoying the sight of the reddish gold Garibaldi.

General Dynamics

General Dynamics Convair was an employment powerhouse in the 40's and 50's. Some 40,000 workers were on its payroll during WWII as it cranked out thousands of B-24 Liberator bombers. In the fifties, its F102 Delta Dagger, the nation's first super-sonic interceptor, was the hot ticket item. Even though its aircraft, Atlas missile, Cruise missile and other space-related tasks would be gone by the early nineties, General Dynamics continues to maintain a strong presence in San Diego with its acquisition of National Steel and Shipbuilding, a prime ship building and repair facility.

But in the fifties, Convair was working overtime to produce the delta winged F102 jet fighter. The jet was being built in a plant on Pacific Highway about a mile from Lindbergh Field. It was always a thrill to watch these jet fighters with their mustard-colored primer take-off from Lindbergh Field. They would roar down the runway then shoot skyward in a steep climb. As sudden as their take-off, they would be out of sight. Today, the former manufacturing plant houses the Navy's Space and Naval Warfare Systems Command (SPAWAR) It was also very exciting to be working for a company whose vice president was Tom Lanphier, the WWII P-38 pilot who shared credit for shooting down Admiral Yamamoto, the Pearl Harbor mastermind, over the Pacific in 1943.

Just a block away from Convair at Lindbergh Field, there was another aircraft plant with historic connections - Ryan Aeronautical. The plane Charles Lindbergh used to make a record shattering crossing of the Atlantic on May 20-21, 1927 was made there. A replica of this plane, the Spirit of St Louis, hangs in San Diego's Air and Space Museum in Balboa Park.

As a buyer for Convair, I had a $10,000 signature authority. Most of my procurements were for spare parts for Convair's 240/340/440 twin engine commercial aircraft. As long as these workhorses remain flying, manufacturers are responsible for supplying the parts needed to keep them flying. This meant maintaining an inventory or the capability to make the parts. Supplying these items became repetitious and boring despite the perks of vendor lunches and parties.

Meanwhile, my evening studies in public administration and political science at San Diego State were preparing me for a career in government administration. It wouldn't be long before I would be making another career shift.

Local Government

San Diego State had just introduced an internship program for graduate students in Public Administration. If I could get someone in the city of San Diego to hire me as an Intern, I could be paid by the city and earn graduate credit at the same time. I tracked down the head of the city's budget department, Les Earnest, just as he was boarding a plane at Lindbergh Field. I made an earnest pitch for an Internship position and he told me to set up an appointment with him when he returned. Meantime, I met with my Convair boss, explained my circumstances, thanked him for the opportunity and departed amicably. I was hired as the city's first public administration intern and assigned to the city budget office.

The budget office was the power center of city administration. This gave me a close up look at such legendary characters as City Manager Hump Campbell and future city managers like Tom Fletcher, Kim Moore and John Locke. It was 1957 and I was assigned work as a budget analyst. This job consisted of reviewing a department's budget request for the coming fiscal year and recommending any appropriate changes. My assignment included review the budget of a couple small departments. But the pace of the work was too slow for me. I didn't fit. I needed something more dynamic. I completed my Internship and applied for an analyst position with the County Welfare department. Here I got an opportunity to be creative and was introduced to the rapidly emerging field of data processing.

It was an era of punched cards and mainframes. It was also an era tied to Fred Taylor's management maxims: flow charts, organization charts, and procedures. It was a time of statistical analysis, time and motion studies and process simplification. I was developing process flow charts that looked like engineering schematics. The flow of every document was tracked to every user. I was expected to streamline and make improvements wherever I could. Streamlining and cost-cutting were the name of the game.

It also included liaison with the County's data processing unit and participation in one of the State's early demonstration of an automated welfare payment system.

Sometimes the efficiency element overrode the human factor. Recommending a typing pool appeared quite efficient but eliminating the social interaction of a heretofore decentralized operation took its toll on worker satisfaction. Bernie used to criticize my work telling me I was making robots out of people. She was right. Turnover in the typing pool was high. It wasn't long before the more humanistic approach of W. Edwards Deming and Peter Drucker took hold. Nor was it long before personal computers and software reduced and, in many cases, eliminated the burden of paperwork and filing.

Homer Detriech, the energetic and personable director of the Welfare Department, taught me the importance of setting priorities and putting first things first. Sid Herzik, the assistant director and my boss, taught me to respect number crunching and the meaning of completed staff work. During this time I also put my college degree to work by securing an Adult teaching credential and teaching US History part-time in the evening for San Diego Adult Education.

Sputnik

On October 4, 1957, as I headed for an evening graduate seminar at San Diego State, I heard some startling news over my car radio. The Russians had just launched the first artificial satellite and it was orbiting the earth. The "beep, beep, beep" sounds emanating from that orbiting satellite filled the airwaves. At that moment, priorities in the

US changed dramatically. We were jolted into a top priority space race with the Soviets. The work already begun on an intercontinental missile was propelled into high gear. San Diego and General Dynamics would be the home of the nation's first intercontinental ballistic missile – the Atlas.

Master's Hang-up

All my coursework for my master's at San Diego State had been completed. Only the thesis remained. I had selected Game Theory for my thesis topic. The theory was abuzz in the political science community for its potential in predicting social, political and economic outcomes. Interest in the field was stimulated by the earlier works of Emile Brel in the 30's and John von Newmann in the 40's. It was a hot topic in Political Science circles in the 50's and prompted me to select it. I even had an acceptance letter to the University of Michigan's doctoral program once my thesis was completed. But I could not get a thesis committee together to oversee my work so the thesis languished and died.

I would resume work on my master's some ten years later at CSU Fullerton. I would have to repeat the entire set of requirements for the master's degree because my earlier coursework was considered out of date having been completed more than seven years earlier. I repeated the coursework. I felt I had a master's degree in spades.

General Dynamics Revisited

Once again I was at a career juncture. My work in government and attraction to Political Science whet my appetite for politics. But, as a government employee, there were some restrictions on partisan activities as spelled out in the Hatch Act. So I left the secure world of government work and went back to the private sector rejoining General Dynamics. This time I was re-hired as a systems analyst in the Astronautics Division.

Just before returning to General Dynamics, we brought our first home in San Diego's Mission Village. Its location was ideal for schools and the Astronautics plant in Kearney Mesa was nearby. Bernie and I were the proud owners of new, three bedroom tract home on a 60x100 foot lot. It cost $18,000. The GI Bill made it possible in much the same way as it made my college education possible.

Meantime, I was having a big problem with the Catholic Church on the issue of birth control. I had several discussions on the matter with our parish priest. Soon after, I remember seriously questioning my faith. I couldn't understand how the mandate of loving one another could square with the pins and needles of pregnancy avoidance if birth control, other than rhythm, was forbidden. I couldn't intellectually accept a virgin birth and a resurrection – key tenets of Catholicism. After years of being steeped in the Catholic faith, I lost it.

Soon after moving into our new home, there was one expense I couldn't resist – the purchase of the Great Books of the Western World. This collection was the brainchild of Mortimer Adler, a philosopher and educator I held in the highest esteem. I had to have that collection. I don't know how many times my wife would point to those books and tell her friends how getting carpeting played second fiddle to those books. She was right. I still have those fifty-two volumes - classic works of science, literature, history and philosophy. Whether I finish reading the entire set is anybody's guess. It will no doubt depend on how long I live. The volume that shows the most wear is the one entitled American State Papers, the Federalist and J.S. Mill. The purchase remains my most prized possession and has made me a lifelong fan of Adler, his philosophy, his ideas and his organizational genius. Two volumes of the set, the Syntopicon, provide an index to the page number and location within the Great Books of an author's position on topics ranging from art, astronomy, life and death to prudence, punishment, war and peace. Adler's influence on me was profound.

Chapter 4

The *SIXTIES*

The sixties were witness to the election of the first Catholic president, the Cuban missile crisis, JFK's assassination, Martin Luther King's I have a Dream speech, Lyndon Johnson's Great Society, Vietnam body counts, Robert Kennedy's assassination, Woodstock, Kent State, Civil Rights marches, activation of the Atlas Missiles system, Alan Shepherd and John Glenn's Mercury flights, the Watts Riots, Nixon's presidency and the first lunar landing.

Space Race

The United States and the Soviet Union were vying for space supremacy. Sputnik had kicked the US space effort into high gear. The world's two dominant nuclear players were racing for space supremacy. Launch vehicles with nuclear warhead capabilities, satellites and manned space craft were part of that race. JFK had already proclaimed a national goal to put a man on the moon before the end of the decade and bring him back safely to earth. The Defense Department, the Air Force and General Dynamics were teamed in developing the Atlas missile, a rocket system that could put satellites as well as men in orbit. It could also deliver a nuclear warhead. The liquid oxygen fueled Atlas missile system would be the nation's first intercontinental ballistic missile system. It could put a nuclear bomb on target some 5,000 miles away. The same rocket would launch our first manned suborbital and orbital space flights. The Mercury Project put Alan Shepherd and John Glenn into the astronaut hall of fame.

I remember watching the manufacture of those bullet-shaped titanium shells moving along the assembly line at the Kearney Mesa plant. At the same time these launch vehicles were being built and their rocket engines tested, silos to house and launch the missiles were being built at Air Force bases around the country. General Dynamics was also managing a tremendous subcontractor effort given the variety and complexity of the ground support equipment. It was one of the most complex integration efforts since WWII. Everything was on a priority basis and everything was being developed concurrently in different parts of the country. As might be expected, there was a lot of retrofitting.

I was part of the management team that had a vital role in streamlining the processes that would expedite the activation of the system. While the Defense Department's effort was underway at flank speed so was NASA's orbital flight program. In February 1962, Marine Colonel John Glenn's Friendship 7 capsule was launched by an Atlas rocket into a 3 orbit pass around the earth. Many more launches from the Cape's Pad 39 would follow.

During this time Dad passed away. He was only 60; the cause, emphysema. It was my first experience with death in my immediate family. It affected me deeply. Shortly after the funeral, my supervisor thought a trip to Cape Canaveral would help snap me out of my depression and restore my spirits. It did. Riding the elevator to the top of Pad 39 where John Glenn recently made history re-charged my battery and got me back in the game.

These were exciting times. Everyone working at General Dynamics felt caught up in something big. On a rare open house, families got to see the missile factory first hand and share the excitement driving their spouses, relatives and friends. Engineering and manufacturing skills were being challenged as never before. Not since WWII had management been challenged with a task of such technical complexity. New airborne and ground support equipment was being designed and built while launch silos were under construction at various Air Force sites. The challenge of ensuring that everything fit properly and reflected the latest engineering requirements was a monumental task. The use of computers for design, manufacturing, logistics and procurement was expanding. The computer-driven information age was emerging.

My family was growing as well. It was during this time that Charlotte and Robin came along; what a joy. I couldn't resist giving them names reflecting my special affection. For Charlotte, it was Charlotte Magoo and later, Charlie Tuna. For Robin, it was Robin Hobgoblin. Ginny and Mark were doing well and getting bigger. But the four year gap between Mark and Ginny and Charlotte and Robin made it seem like two sets of families.

Meanwhile back at Astronautics, I was part of the team responsible for configuration management as well as rapid-response to design and manufacturing requirements. With so many different technical specialties involved and the pressure to activate launch sites quickly, the bureaucratic structures of an earlier age had to go. Communication lines had to be shortened. Departments had to plan and work concurrently rather than in silo or isolated fashion. This led to the formation of an interdisciplinary team that could work elbow-to-elbow in the same room and expedite the implementation of design and manufacturing changes. A new department would be created responsible for configuration management and change control. Engineering changes could now find their way into the manufacturing process in record time.

Several individuals spearheaded this effort but two individuals in particular had lead roles – Herb Courington who would head the new Configuration Management Department and Jim Boggus who would lead the Management Systems effort. I was Jim's sidekick in developing the policies and procedures that the Vice President and General Manager, Jim Dempsey would approve. This new effort resulted in key individuals from different departments being physically co-located in one, central work area. All changes to the system were reviewed in roundtable fashion and all participants had decision-making authority. Changes could be implemented in record time. This organization broke down the insulation of a departmental or silo mentality into one that was mission-oriented and cut across all departmental lines. All the top talent necessary to accomplish tasks in record time were within easy earshot of one another. A matrix-style organization emerged from this arrangement. Departments would continue to reflect their assigned functional responsibilities while program managers would draw on departmental talent to support their mission. All this was taking place at a time when launch silos and ground support equipment were being designed and built as Atlas missiles were coming off the assembly line. It was a marvel of systems engineering and integration. Keeping everyone on the same page as changes and problems were being resolved at different locations throughout the country was no easy task.

Once the new Configuration Management department was up and running, I was assigned to the Centaur program, a new, higher energy rocket that used liquid hydrogen as a propellant rather than the liquid oxygen like the Atlas. The same procedures used to manage the configuration of the Atlas missile were applied. I also introduced a series of problem resolution forums that created a free style exchange of conditions interfering with smooth and efficient operations.

These forums were conducted on Saturday mornings. Attendance was voluntary. Skeptics doubted anyone would show up. But the number attending was gratifying. Anyone could air complaints or suggest ways to improve operations. The proceedings and the recommendations were summarized and reported to top management immediately after. Corrective actions and organizational changes were implemented expeditiously.

Then there were lighter moments. At one of the regular program reviews where PERT charts (performance evaluation reporting technique) were used to track the status of critical missile items, a bizarre event took place. Schedules for critical items had to be met. Chang, the program manager and a former air wing commander in Chiang Kai-shek's Nationalist air force, took his cigar from his mouth and, in his curt, Chinese- accented way, started in.

"Alright. Let's get started. I want to know if the completion dates for the critical items on the chart are still good."

A few days earlier, the staff decided to test Chang's sense of humor. Buying a tin of Chinese fortune cookies, they painstakingly opened the cookies and replaced the fortunes with slips of paper containing updated shipping dates for each of the critical items. The cookies were glued back and resealed in the cookie tin.

"Chang", one of the staffers replied, "we're having a hell of time getting reliable answers out of our vendors. We've resorted to fortune cookies."

With that, someone slid the tin of fortune cookies towards Chang. Someone next to him just happened to have a can opener, intercepted the can, opened it and dumped the contents on the table. The cookies were passed around the table to staffers who began breaking them open and reading the slips.

"Hey", look at what I've got. Here's a delivery schedule for critical item number such and such." Others chimed in more delivery schedule updates as the fortune cookies were split open. All the data was up-to-the-minute and accurate. The PERT (Performance Evaluation and Reporting Technique) charts were updated accordingly. Everyone, including Chang, had a good laugh.

One thing I liked about my job more than anything else was the challenge and variety. My job was to work myself out of a job by helping departments solve problems that crossed departmental lines. I enjoyed access to managers and workers throughout the company. My final procedural agreements bore the signature of the Vice President and General Manager. Nor was there any fear about running out of work. Process improvements in a company the size of General Dynamics were never ending. I liked the comprehensive nature of the job and helping departments orchestrate needed improvements.

The importance of our work on the nation's first intercontinental missile system created an atmosphere of excitement and comeraderie. Luncheons to celebrate operational achievements, promotions and anniversaries were frequent. Parties over the Christmas and New Year holidays were memorable. It was a time when WWII was not that distant and many employees were veterans of that war and Korea. At one of our Christmas parties I was the center of attention in a small group. I was describing the near destruction of a model P40 fighter I bought as a Christmas gift for my son Mark. Someone joined our circle just as I was using my arms and hands to describe the angle of attack when the model plane crashed.

"My God, man. How did you walk away from that one!" He had come into the conversation at the tail end and thought I was talking about a real experience.

"I didn't. I bought the farm." I replied. You can imagine the laughter that followed.

Politics

During those heady days of missile building, raising a family, going to graduate school and teaching, my interest in politics was also keen. In the late fifties and early sixties, grassroots politics in California was at an all- time high. For a few years, grassroots action was a deciding factor in California's partisan elections. The California Democratic Council had set in motion door-to-door campaigning and collecting Dollars for Democrats. It was giving the average voter a sense of participation in the political process and stimulating the rise of neighborhood Democratic Clubs. Republicans had their own grassroots counterpart, the Republican Associates.

The California Democratic Council was organizing regional conferences where debates on national and international policies were taking place engaging delegates from San Diego to northern California. Presentations and position papers were as intense and real as Congressional committee hearings. At the local level, club members were endorsing candidates in Democratic races and becoming a decisive factor in candidate victories. Local club endorsements were making a real difference in candidate victories.

I unsuccessfully sought a pre-primary endorsement for an Assembly seat in new 76th Assembly District. A pre-primary endorsement meant a primary win. These pre-primaries took place in open conventions with speeches and votes. I sold my prized De Walt power saw to cover my campaign literature costs. One of my key advocacies at the time was construction of a rapid transit system. The system would take advantage of the latest technology and look like the Disneyland monorail. It would take advantage of the freeway center-divide and whiz by the frustratingly slow freeway traffic. It has taken over fifty years but its looks like we now have the beginning of a real rapid transit system in the works.

In the meantime I remained active in political activities and was appointed to an Assembly District Council slot by Sumner Alpert, a level headed regional official with the Democratic Council and an executive at the local Solar Corporation. Because I was well known to voters in my neighborhood, I was elected twice to the Democratic Central Committee for San Diego County. Meantime, it was a heyday of Democratic ascendancy throughout the State. Governor Pat Brown, Controller Alan Cranston, Senator Hugo Fisher, Assemblyman Jim Mills all benefitted from the support from the California Democratic Council. But nothing fueled the fires of political participation at the grassroots level as the presidential candidacy of John F. Kennedy. I remember him making a campaign speech in front of the Grant Hotel in downtown San Diego. His words, vigor and good looks were a winning combination.

I used my many political contacts to advantage in my Adult Education history and government classes. Knowing so many local political figures, I had little difficulty getting them to appear as guest speakers before my students. Their appearance enriched the classroom experience. These practitioners conveyed the reality of government. They also served to encourage students to engage personally in our governing processes.

Unfortunately, the grassroots movement of the early sixties petered out not long after the Kennedy victory. Many of the California Democratic Council leaders now held elective office and were immersed in their new jobs at the State and national capitols. The loss of their personal influence at the local level, however, weakened the grassroots movement. Policy and priority squabbles further splintered the movement. But the echoes of "ask not what your country can do for you but what you can do for your country" still lingered and so did the gigantic challenge of putting a man on the moon by the end of the decade. But by the mid sixties, the popular grassroots movement of the California Democratic

Council was waning. But this waning was a product of its own success in accomplishing its mission – the election of Democratic political leaders. Newly elected leaders owed their election victories in large part to the California Democratic Council. The same leaders now held legislative and governing posts in Sacramento and Washington. Ironically, local organizations were weakened by their very success. Many California Democratic Council leaders were now serving in State and national capitals. Their absence on the local scene and the policy and priority differences within the party on the local level tended to weaken the organization's coherence. The California Democratic Council that had been such an effective force in the early sixties was fading.

Cuban Missile Crisis

Up until 1962, no period in American's history was as intense and dangerous as the Cuban Missile Crisis of October 1962. The Soviet positioning of nuclear tipped warheads in Castro's Communist Cuba brought America to a state of readiness it hadn't experienced since Pearl Harbor. President Kennedy spoke to the nation and warned of the crisis and our position. Bomb shelters were being built and supermarket shelves were being cleared as people hastened to buy and store food. Civilian residents of Guantanamo Bay were evacuated, Marines were at the ready to invade Cuba and the Air Force and Navy were ready for nuclear war. A quarantine of weapons being shipped into Cuba was in effect. We were eyeball-to-eyeball with the Soviet Union. Then there was a breakthrough on the diplomatic front and the Soviets withdrew their missiles. It was not until decades later that the American people were let in on the deal that led to the Soviet missile withdrawal. At the time, the US had missiles stationed in Turkey and aimed at the Soviet Union. We agreed to remove these missiles in return for the Soviets removing theirs from Cuba.

About the mid- sixties, work on the Atlas missile program was also winding down although the launch vehicle would continue as a workhorse for various missions and tests. But people were getting lay-off notices. Even those remaining on payrolls were encouraged to seek new jobs. It was time to find work with another contractor with defense dollars.

McDonnell Aircraft

I had several interviews with different defense and space contractors at the time including Minneapolis Honeywell, Hewlett-Packard and Atlantic Research. I took a systems analyst position with Atlanta Research in Duarte, California but after just a few months on the job got caught in another defense contract cutback. I then accepted a job offer from McDonnell Aircraft in St. Louis.

"Don't worry. I'll be able to work my way back to California in a matter of months."

With these assuring words, I left behind a wife, three daughters and a son to work for McDonnell Aircraft in St. Louis. I was certain I could get back to Southern California in less than a year. As it worked out, I was back in California in less than eight months. The move minimized interruptions in Ginny and Mark's schooling and whatever routines Bernie had going for Charlotte and Robin. Besides, Bernie was not keen on leaving California. Our new Buick station wagon would give her all the mobility she needed.

Once in St Louis, I bought an old Chevy for $100, rented a room in a private residence in St. Charles and reported for duty at nearby McDonnell Aircraft. I would be working in the Engineering Department as a program analyst reviewing contract requirements, ensuring contract compliance and working on new proposals.

The hot products at McDonnell at this time included the F4 Phantom jet and the Gemini space capsule. Vietnam was heating up and the F4 was just starting to see action in that theatre. The Gemini space capsule was a two man version of the single man Mercury capsule. Gemini was designed to study the endurance of astronauts in a zero gravity environment and their ability to work in space outside the capsule. Gemini would be the forerunner to the three man Apollo vehicle which would make the lunar landing.

Part of the excitement of working at McDonnell was to hear the voice of Mr. McDonnell over the company loudspeakers when he made firsthand reports of his visits to the Cape for Gemini launch events.

"This is Old Mac addressing the team. This morning I enjoyed a low residue breakfast with our astronauts who will soon be blasting off here at the Cape ......"

He would then go on to describe the things that were happening around him. This report from the CEO was a real "make you feel proud" moment for McDonnell employees especially those who seldom got to meet the individuals who would be using the final product of their labors.

For awhile I filled my nights with a part time job as a salesman for Sears and as a warehouse guard for a private security firm on weekends. The warehouse job was ideal for preparing resumes and sending them back to California. But another diversion soon captured my attention.

Dancing on the Mississippi

Just down the street from where I lived in St. Charles, there was a ballroom. I always had an interest in dancing but never pursued it. Now an opportunity to do so was literally at my doorstep. As in many dance environments, women tend to outnumber men. On my first visit to that ballroom, a blond-haired woman who was an excellent dancer latched onto me. It was just the luck of the draw. Estelle was not only one of the best dancers in the place but the leader of a small group of dance enthusiasts.

At the time, my dancing was halting and lacked confidence. But joining Estelle's entourage overcame my dancing deficiencies in short order. Being part of her entourage meant going to dance classes and practicing. With two to three months of weekly instruction by a ballroom professional with a Spanish accent, my dancing began to improve. As my proficiency grew, so did my enjoyment. I was hooked. I was now dancing the foxtrot, the swing, the cha cha, the samba, the rhumba, and the waltz.

A dancing routine had settled in - classes, practice and Sunday afternoons on the Mississipp Delta Queen. The Delta Queen environment was interesting. Like many dancers, I wasn't much of a drinker but in Missouri you could bring you own alcohol aboard the ship. However, you had to buy your mixes on board. Dancers are notoriously light drinkers when dancing so the sale of non-alcoholic beverages was the right match for a dancing crowd.

Estelle was a great dancer and a very independent woman. She had her own dry cleaning business. She told me that when she started her business she knew nothing about it. But she hired someone who knew the business and learned from her. She also had a daughter in San Diego and planned to visit her soon.

Meanwhile, the resumes I had been sending back to California aerospace firms connected. I flew back to California for two job interviews. One was with the Aerospace Corporation in San Bernardino and the other with Douglas Aircraft in Long Beach. This was a fork-in-the-road decision point. At one point, I had an employee badge for both Douglas and Aerospace. After interviewing with Hal Norman of the Aerospace Corporation, I chose to join the Aerospace Corporation and returned the Douglas badge and money advance. My interview with Aerospace' Hal Norman took place at his home in Riverside. It was August 1965. The Watts Riots were in full swing. But the joy of reuniting with my family overshadowed the turmoil in LA and even the excitement of a new job.

The Aerospace Corporation

The Aerospace Corporation is a non-profit think tank for the Air Force Systems Command. Its job is to provide systems engineering, technical support, contract performance statements and strategic planning. The corporate headquarters is in El Segundo but its major re-entry physics activities took place in a new building just outside the gates of Norton Air Force base in San Bernardino. My job had two major tracks. One was preparing a monthly report for Pentagon officials on the status of weapon systems under development by major Air Force contractors across the country. The report had to be put into language readily understood by those not familiar with the current engineering and physics jargon. This was quite an experience and challenge for me. It meant spending considerable time with individual engineers breaking down their technical jargon into plain, easily understood English. The other element involved coordinating the review of unsolicited proposals and formulating a response.

In addition to the monthly report for Pentagon brass, I also attended the General Manager's progress review meetings. At these reviews, all the main players in engineering, re-entry physics, fusing and weapons systems made presentations summarizing the progress and problems of major contractors. Aerospace program managers would define the progress and problems being experienced by key national defense contractors. Ensuing discussion engaged the entire technical staff. Suggestions were offered for problem resolution. The input from these highly educated and multi-disciplined staff really impressed me. From time to time there would be disagreement and bruised egos but overall it managed to focus the experience and skill of the whole organization on specific problems It was also chilling to be present as staff members discussed the kill ratio of nuclear blasts at various altitudes. This was a time when underground testing of nuclear devices was still in progress.

Redlands

Redlands bordered San Bernardino and was only a 10 minute drive from work. At the time, the housing market was in a bust cycle. Tracts of homes were abandoned in mid-construction. In San Diego, however, the rental market was good and we were able to rent our home to good tenants.

We found a two story, five bedroom, 3 bath home with a 3 car garage for $37,000. The schools in the area were good and we were smack in the middle of orange country. When in bloom, the scent of the orange blossoms was overwhelming. Giant palm trees lined the front of our house. When the winter winds blew, they would sway and bend. I was always afraid those trees would topple but their roots held. We had great views of snow capped San Gorgonio and Mount Baldy. At night we could see the lights as far away as the Pomona Valley and the LA basin.

We made frequent trips to the local mountain resorts including Running Springs, Big Bear and Lake Arrowhead. Ginny enjoyed ice skating at Blue Jay and, for awhile, Ginny and I took roller dance lessons together at the local skating rink. We both passed our bronze level, roller dancing test. As a family we also made frequent trips to our favorite coastal haunts like Newport Beach. Trips to Newport were usually capped with a stop at the area's favorite fish restaurant, the Crab Cooker. We enjoyed the clam chowder, bread sticks and fish dinners. The kids also liked the free salt water taffy the Crab Cooker offered its customers digging out a handful from the big glass jar near the entrance when leaving.

Ballroom Dancing

Our Redlands residence stimulated a whole new set of interests for the kids as well as Bernie and myself. Ginny took to horseback riding and the piano. Mark joined the Redlands YMCA swimming team and his awards began plastering his bedroom walls. He was also showing an interest in martial arts. Bernie enrolled Charlotte and Robin in ballet classes. I put physical conditioning, swimming and handball into my weekly routine by joining the San Bernardino YMCA. I met some great handball players there who made me very conscious of the differences among A, B and C level players. I was not an A player but some A levels liked to use me for warm-up. This helped my game. I also met some great body builders, one of whom made the cover of Muscle magazine.

My dancing interest came to the fore but not before we resolved a foot problem that had plagued Bernie for some time. She had a plantar wart imbedded in the ball of her foot that caused her great pain and had to be shaved down monthly. It would definitely interfere with her dancing. Something more permanent had to be done. The permanent solution required some bone surgery that she was reluctant to have done. But dancing was the magic motivator. A Doctor Forest Young of Redlands, a noted specialist in a bone shortening procedure, performed a successful operation giving Bernie years of pain free dancing. Now we were able to share our dance enthusiasm with some fellow workers.

I managed to get Aerospace to sponsor an employee ballroom dance class. We were able to hire a professional dance instructor who brought a group of us up to speed on a number of different dances including the fox trot, waltz, swing, cha cha and rumba. After a couple weeks of lessons we felt it was time to display our dancing skills at some local night spots. About eight of us would descend on a local club that had a dance floor and live music. We enjoyed displaying our new dancing skills. Our dancers were very comfortable on the night club scene especially New York transplants like engineer Herb Cohen and his wife Toby and scientist Sid Katz and his wife Rose. Herb was recognized for his dipping skill at the end of a dance and became known as "Herb, the Dipper".

As our circle of dance enthusiasts expanded, we got to know other instructors and dancing venues in both San Bernardino and Riverside. One standout instructor was a Mr. Whiteside of Riverside. His execution of the waltz was a joy to behold. His posture and fluidity of movement set a standard we could only hope to attain. But the inland empire was more oriented towards western and country music than ballroom. We soon gravitated towards square dancing.

Square Dancing

Square dancing added a new dimension to our dancing portfolio. Some friends of ours at Aerospace arranged for a square dance instructor to join our dance activities. This marked the beginning of our square dance association with local clubs.

The Inland Empire had a strong presence on the country and square dance scene, much more so than ballroom. After we completed a square dance course, we gravitated from one square dance club to another until we found the one (s) we preferred. Our favorite club was the B Sharps founded and directed by Larry Ward, a legendary instructor. Larry was also a great showman. His personality was reflected in the pizazz of his black Cadillac featuring steer horns across the grill. He was the square dance equivalent of a rock star. My last Internet check showed Larry still active on the square dance scene and conducting classes in Nevada.

Larry's dancers were standouts everywhere. They were noted for their precision and smoothness. You could only get into B Sharps by invitation, a peer screening that kept our dancing at a level high. We were invited to join and met weekly for Larry's Inland Empire workshop in Yucaipa, a small city bordering Redlands. We had more fun dancing at Larry's workshops than at a regular club dance. The Yucaipa dancing venue was great, a huge wooden floor atop a Von's supermarket. It was "Square 'em up, gents go left and girls go right, up to the middle and back, doe-si-doe, bend the line, make a wave, gents pick up your pretty little Taw...." There were usually about ten squares in motion at all times.

Square dancing also involved looking the part. That meant a new outfit. Unlike the ballroom scene where office attire was commonplace, square dancing called for a western look. For the men it meant boots, levi's, plaid shirts, string ties, western style belt buckles and western hats. For the women it meant bouffant skirts and flat soled shoes. Footwear, however, was the most important item. For men, the lightweight Northern Star dancing boot was preferable to a regular boot. This lightweight boot made all the difference in comfort and step execution. For women, a heel-less, slipper-style shoe was most popular. Occasionally, some dancers would wear a Capezio shoe with a short Cuban heel. The capezio, however, was more prominent on the folk dance scene.

Dad with Robin, Char and Mark

Our prima ballerina Ginny

In addition to the dress code, another element, the most important of all, was the dance floor surface. Wood is best because of its resiliency especially when laid over materials that provide additional cushioning like rubber. Tile surfaces are slippery and conducive to slips and leg fatigue. Concrete and asphalt are the worst and should be avoided. Such surfaces are tiring, dangerous for the knees and will wear out the soles of your shoes faster than anything.

After a square dance workshop or club dance there was nothing as enjoyable as the pizza that followed at a local watering hole. Dancing can work up an appetite and sharing pizza after a dance hits the spot. A dedicated lot, dancers usually manage to find the time and money to keep up with their hobby. And, many dancers seem to be blessed with longevity. Like MacArthur's reference to a WWI ballad during his farewell address to Congress, dancers, like old soldiers, never die; they just fade away.

While working at Aerospace, I also conducted reading classes for adults as a faculty adjunct for San Bernardino Adult Education. These classes were for adults who could not read. What a contrast to my day job. My days were spent in the company of highly educated scientists and engineers while some of my nights were spent in the company of adults unable to read or write. It opened my eyes to the reality of illiteracy in this country. It meant teaching at the most basic level – the alphabet, pronunciation of letters and letter combinations. It is amazing how an adult can speak perfectly fluent English yet hide an inability to read or write. But the students were motivated. If they wanted promotion they would have to handle paperwork. This meant knowing how to read.

Mark's Seizure

Meanwhile, my idyllic life in Redlands was called up short with a phone call from the Loma Linda Medical center.

"Mr. Byron, this is Dr. Hopkins at the Loma Linda Medical Center. Your son Mark had a seizure at school today. He is here at the hospital and resting comfortably. We have him on medication and he can come home in a day or so." Bernie had received a similar call just before I did. We both went directly to the hospital.

Weeks of adjustment followed. We had to learn about epilepsy, the different types of seizures - grand mal and petit - how to manage a seizure episode, how to minimize stress for Mark, the importance of medication like dilantin and how to reconcile ourselves with Mark's condition. It was difficult for me to accept. Bernie and I searched through family histories and genetic predispositions. We couldn't find anything. Mark did not have any memory of his seizure. . But Mark would eventually learn how to recognize signs that a seizure was about to occur. Slurred speech was one of the tell-tale signs.

After a few weeks, things at home and school got back to normal. Meanwhile, there was talk of relocating certain company operations back to the corporate headquarters at El Segundo. I would be a casualty of this consolidation but rehired by another firm almost immediately.

Folk Dancing

Meanwhile, another long lasting dance association was beginning– folk dance. On one of frequent Sunday jaunts to the coast, we often visited one of our favorite sites - Balboa Park. The park was always a favorite for locals and tourists alike. Adjacent to the world famous San Diego zoo, it featured natural history, science, art and aerospace museums, an outdoor organ pavilion, a group of cottages representing different nations, an outdoor theatre, a large gymnasium, a miniature railway, a Japanese garden and photography exhibit, a couple of restaurants and one of largest botanical exhibits in the State. The Spanish style architecture was designed for a 1915 world fair celebrating the opening of the Panama Canal.

Balboa Park was also noted for its spacious halls ideal for dancing and the preferred site of many different dance groups. While visiting the park one Sunday, we came across a group of dancers moving to unfamiliar music and dressed in a variety of costumes of different nations. We were impressed with the variety of physical connection patterns the dancers assumed – hands or shoulders and belts as the dancers moved to the music in a circular pattern. The wooden dance floor was one of the largest in San Diego county. As we watched and talked to some of the dancers, we learned something about the dance origins. The music came from Serbia, Bulgaria, Croatia, Romania, Greece, Hungary and Poland. Although many of the dancers were older there were enough young dancers to get Charlotte and Robin's attention. One, in fact, was a former associate of mine from my earlier work experience at General Dynamics

During the course of our conversations we met a young couple from Riverside, Sol and Suzy. Both were affiliated with the University and they invited us to join their folk dance club. This marked the beginning of our entrée to the folk dance scene. I also recognized someone I knew from my former days at General Dynamics. John Hancock was an excellent dancer. His participation enhanced my interest in this dance form.

Dancing at the University of Riverside was ideal. It was done in a large room with a wooden floor and mirrored walls. During the day, it was used for ballet training. We began attending the Thursday evening folk dance which Sol and Suzy led. They also taught a folk dance at the beginning of each session. We brought Charlotte and Robin along with us rather than hire a baby sitter. Although only 7and 5 years old, the exposure caught them at a very impressionable age. They must have learned by osmosis since they seemed more intent in amusing themselves than paying attention to the instruction. But they obviously absorbed the folk rhythms and body movements. Later, they would be instructors, the performers and the leaders within the folk dance community.

The more we engaged in folk dancing, the more sensitive we became to the richness of the music and the variations in the dance styles from different regions, villages and countries. Folk songs and dances are integral to the culture of all nations. There are so many different dances worldwide that even the most proficient of teachers would find it difficult to know them all. The dances we performed were primarily from the Balkans and Middle East. The nations included Serbia, Croatia, Macedonia, Bulgaria, Romania, Greece, Turkey, Armenia and Israel. The more popular couple dances were usually associated with Hungary, Sweden, Poland and Russia.

Remembering and pronouncing the names of the dances were often more challenging than executing the dance. I often found it easier to do a dance than remember its name. My wife and daughters, however, had a facility for remembering both the name and the dance. The music of most different nationalities have distinctive rhythms and sounds. The music can also reflect a cultural overlap especially in border areas. After many months of folk dancing, I was usually able to identify the origin of most popular folk dances.

Those of us living in Southern California were fortunate to have so many master teachers from Europe attracted to this area. Some were members of outstanding performing groups who defected while touring the US. Europe's loss was America's gain. These master teachers energized the folk dance movement in California years before détente.

Anaheim

Within a week of leaving the Aerospace Corporation, I was working at Northrop in Anaheim. I was assigned the oversight of the manufacture of fuselage sections for Boeing's new 747. This entailed identifying problems and assisting in their resolution. It was fascinating to see how coils of cold aluminum would be taken from freezers, placed on conveyors and squeezed to different thicknesses by machine tools called Yoder Rolls. The variations in thickness provided greater strength where needed and reduced weight where less strength was required.

After months of commuting from Redlands, I discovered a new job opportunity in the city of Anaheim. The manager of that city, Keith Murdoch, was interested in applying aerospace management techniques to local government operations. He was interested in program budgeting, teamwork and management information systems. My aerospace experience involving the systems approach and program management, my background in local government and my graduate work in public administration fit the bill. I was interviewed, offered the job and, within two weeks, heading up the City's new Administrative Research department. I reported directly to the City Manager.

City of Anaheim

It was a growth time for the city of Anaheim. Disneyland's recent opening in Anaheim put the city on the map. A new Angel baseball stadium with Gene Autry Enterprises at the helm gave Anaheim a major league baseball team. A new convention center across the street from Disneyland had just swung into operation. The Convention Center was financed under a joint-powers agreement between the city of Anaheim and the Anaheim School District. It didn't take long for commercial interests to move in with hotels and restaurants. These developments meant more revenue for the city but also more service requirements and traffic controls.

Disneyland, the stadium and the convention center put Anaheim on the map big time. The value of land in the Disneyland area skyrocketed. Clean industries like Rockwell, Warner-Lambert, Northrop and Winnebago were in place. The city already had a golf course and prided itself on its parks. Its annexation of land in the Santa Ana Canyon would mean re-zoning from agriculture to residential thereby increasing the value of the land substantially. The city manager, Keith Murdoch, looked on the city as a club that had just the right mix of housing, industry, entertainment and services; an environment attractive to clean industry and investment. I remember Keith telling me on one occasion that the thing that made annexations in the Santa Ana Canyon so feasible was access to sewer lines. Anaheim's sewer line network was readily accessible to new lines.

It didn't take long take long for the City Council and City Manager to give me my first major assignment as head of Administrative Research. I was to undertake an analysis and make a report on the anticipated economic impact of a new Stadium and Convention Center on the city's coffers and operations. The study was to be built around the economic hub that Disneyland had already created. Now with a Stadium and Convention Center added to the mix, the task of developing projections as to population, tourist accommodations, traffic, revenue and expenses became a high priority project. It would call for best estimates of new hotel and restaurant construction, street improvements, police and fire protection. It would mean determining revenue potential from sales and hotel room taxes. When the report was finished and distributed around the country, it wasn't long before all available real estate in the vicinity of these new facilities was bought up. Harbor Boulevard and Katella Avenue became the nexus of high rise hotels, restaurants and bars. The cash registers would be ringing and associated revenue would find its way into the city's coffers.

Anaheim Hills

Meantime, we sold our houses in Redlands and San Diego. Our new house was another two story, five bedroom, 3 bath home located in the new Anaheim Hills area in the Santa Ana Canyon. Until a new tract opened behind us, our backyard was bordered with orange groves. As its name implies, oranges were a major crop with strawberries running a close second. In fact, in the early years of the State's organization, naming the county was a toss- up between Orange County or Strawberry County. But the sixties were a heyday for housing developers. The whirr of bulldozers could be heard from dawn to dusk as orange groves made way for homes.

We got the kids enrolled in school and Bernie was busy with the house. We also got Ginny a horse She named the horse Baby and boarded her at a stable not far from our house. There was, however, one drawback. The stable did not have running water. We had to haul tubs of water to Baby's boarding site every day. But Ginny enjoyed riding Baby especially up our street. She would even put Baby in our backyard. I can remember coming home on more than one occasion to find Baby practically in our living room. But it wasn't long before we put the house off-limits to horses. Baby was sold soon after.

We also had a big Irish Setter named Big Red. We bought him in Redlands and brought him with us to Anaheim. Big Red was Bernie's faithful home companion. As a member of the canine sporting group, he proved it every time we took him to the beach. He loved chasing seagulls. He also loved to plop in any muddy hole he could find especially after a bath. As best we could tell, his romps ended with a collision with a car on nearby Highway 57. We missed Big Red.

We also had two cats, favorites with Charlotte and Robin. Both were females and we had our share of kittens. We always had a hard time keeping track of one of the mother cats and her kittens. She would constantly move her kittens to different places. We never knew where to find them. I don't know how many times we had to form search parties to find them. Closets and bureau drawers were favorite hideaways.

Program Budgeting

After completing the Economic Impact report for the city, I moved directly into program budgeting. At the time, only a few local governments had made the conversion. Most were using the traditional departmental-line item budget. Philadelphia had converted to the program budget format and so had County of Orange. Program budgeting allowed you to get a better handle on specific objectives and related costs. Instead of viewing a city as a collection of departments with specific functions, policy makers could focus their attention on major issues or goals and commit resources in a more focused manner. A program manager would be assigned who could draw on whatever resources were needed from different departments. It introduced new measures for collecting costs and establishing performance measures. Program budgeting shifted emphasis from a department to a mission. This was a hard sell for city personnel who were used to thinking in terms of a departmental budget. To accommodate the culture, we developed two versions of the budget – a traditional line-item, departmental budget and a budget that was program-oriented..

My biggest supporter in this budgeting effort was Maxine Waters, an analyst in the county's Chief Administrator's office. She had worked with the Chief Administrator when he was the commanding officer of San Diego's 11th Naval District. Together they applied their military experience in program budgeting to the county and it was working well. Along the lines of military service expectations, I had an early-on opportunity to bring a new-hire into my organization. The individual I chose didn't match the usual profile but was someone I thought could adjust to new environment quickly and get a job done professionally. The individual I selected, Bill Butcher, was a recently retired Army colonel who had served in Vietnam. The usual new hire profile was a younger and a newly minted graduate from a Public Administration master's program. But in this case, we had a real job to do, there was a development fever in the air and our assignment had to be tackled with dispatch and depth. Bill Butcher turned out to be an excellent choice. Bill was a real help in getting our job done but I had some selling to do.

Program budgeting was a culture shock to local government. City officials were used to looking at budgets on a department by department basis rather than programs and missions. Neither did their budgets have targets or effectiveness measures. For example, if a city wanted to undertake a beautification program and targeted specific streets and pedestrian walkways, several departments would have to co-operate in the venture - Public Works, Water, Parks and Recreation, Police etc. Teamwork was natural and integral. Most cities already working this way without all the new terminology. A program orientation simply highlights why we do what we do, provides for progress measurements and collects costs accordingly. This is something most managers do instinctively.

We accounted for program costs using estimates from the affected departments. A simple percentage estimate of salaries and resources was used initially. The departments would estimate how much in terms of salary and resources they were uisng to achieve a program objective. These estimates were consolidated to provide an overall amount being allocated to a given program. These expenditures were related to the milestones established for achieving policy objectives.

At this time we were also competing for grants to build a state-of-the-art municipal information system. The building block for the information system was land. The County Assessor, as custodian of the land and its parcels held the information base on which the information system would be built. That information would include land values, property taxes, census data, inventories, etc. Cities were forming consortia of universities and private companies to compete for funds from the federal Housing and Urban Development to develop such a system. We were teamed with the University of Southern California and a major private consulting firm. Although we did not win a major grant in the competition, we did win a smaller grant for the police information systems.

One of my ultimate goals was to equip the city council chambers with a large video screen on which the current status of programs budgets and achievements could be displayed for the council and members of the public. The display would include the charts and graphs reflecting performance and budget status as well as camera footage of the progress being made in the field. At this time, however, hardware capabilities exceeded software availability. Today's hardware and software put this presentation capability in the hands of any city wanting it.

My experience in developing new systems for the city became the basis of two articles I developed for the Journal of Systems Management. One article was on program budgeting; the other on municipal information systems. My Anaheim experience also provided the impetus for completing my master's degree in Public Administration. I had to repeat thirty six units because my prior thirty units of graduate work was considered outdated since it was completed more than seven years ago. In the process, I also acquired a Life Credential for teaching Public Administration, Political Science and History in community colleges, adult education and grades K-12. Over the years, I would get a lot of use out of this credential.

Meanwhile, back at City Hall, I felt I had gone as far as I could go in terms of program budgeting and a municipal information system. I requested the Manager to put me into a consulting role and he did. My final product for Anaheim and my first task as a consultant was to prepare a report summarizing the city's program budgeting status along with estimates of future acquisition costs for related hardware and software. About this time, the articles I developed earlier on program budgeting and information systems were published in the Journal of Systems Management.

The Intersection

My dancing hobby was a great stress reliever and a key source of family entertainment during those busy days at city hall. Our dancing frequency picked up as we joined local folk dance clubs like the Orange County Folk and Laguna Beach Folk Dancers. But the real frosting on the cake was dancing at the Intersection.

The Intersection was the focal point for folk dancers throughout the Southland. This café was located on Temple Street just off the Hollywood Freeway. It was the most stimulating dancing center in

Southern California. The dances, primarily line dances, were from a variety of countries primarily the Balkans. Different nights featured dances from particular countries. One night it would be Serbian, another Bulgarian, another Romanian, another Greek, another Israeli, another Turkish and another, a mixer. The participants themselves added to the excitement. Some were hippie types, some professional and professorial, some ethnic and many simply dance enthusiasts. Overall, these dancers were the most avid and proficient in the area.

The Intersection's layout was ideally suited to its activities even though the parking lot was too small and you had to use side streets. When you entered, a kitchen area was on your right and to your immediate front, just past a counter and cash register, there were steps leading up to the dance floor. We usually went as a family except for Ginny and Mark. Sometimes a fellow club member would accompany us. My family was usually large enough to be the leading element in many of the line dance lines. I was partial to Greek dancing which resulted in my visiting the Intersection solo on nights Athan was teaching. My family seemed to prefer dances from Bulgaria, Romania, Macedonia and Serbia.

The Intersection featured an upstairs dining area where you could look down on the dancers as you ate. The ethnic composition of the customers and dancers was as diverse as the music. The presence of grey beards playing backgammon at side tables as dancers circled the floor gave the Intersection a European ambience.

Most of the credit for the surge in popularity of folk dancing, in addition to the arrival of so many star performers from the Balkans – defectors or otherwise - goes to Athan Karras and the Intersection. Athan founded this cafe with a partner Rudy Dannes. Another prominent figure during this folk dance renaissance was John Filcich, a strong promoter of Serbian music. John owned and operated Festival Records on Pico Boulevard. He was also the founder of San Francisco's annual Kolo Festival. But for sheer charisma and excitement, few could match Athan and his Greek dances. While we may have chided Athan for his never ending variations of the same dance, we couldn't fault his creativity or enthusiasm. He taught me many dances including such personal favorites as Makadonikos Horo, Kritiko Syrto, Sousta, Hassapiko and

Hassapiserviko. Athan passed away in 2010, a profound loss to all who knew and loved him.

Robin and Bulgaria

Robin had the unique experience of spending a summer in Bulgaria with members of a State-sponsored Bulgarian Folk Dance group. The invite came while we were hosting a party for the group at our Anaheim home. After some soul searching, Bernie and I agreed to let her go. The experience enhanced Robin's folk dance credentials considerably. I was amazed at the Bulgarian proficiency she acquired in such a brief period of time.

Aman

Aman was a nationally acclaimed folk dance troupe reknowned for its artistry, authenticity, and precision performances. The Intersection was a second home for their dancers. Many of the members taught there and kept the dancing level high. To be accepted into Aman, you had to audition. If you qualified, you had to attend rigorous practice sessions and participate in nation-wide tours. Charlotte and Robin were accepted into the troupe, participated in the practices and had to be excused from school on many occasions to participate in out of State tours. As might be expected, the Aman dancers developed a special bond among themselves. Over the years they have held reunions to keep that bond intact.

Dance Teachers

The Intersection featured a number of outstanding teachers offering top level instructions a variety of Balkan and Middle Eastern dances. These included Ruby Vuceta (until her untimely death in an auto accident while vacationing in Europe), Athan Karras, Dick Oakes, Billy Burke, Barry Glass, Paul Sheldon and Charlotte and Robin Byron. These names are standouts within the folk dance community and most were members of Aman.

One Notable Character

Nick

One of the more memorable patrons of the Intersection was Nick, a vintage Greek dancer with a white, handlebar moustache. Nick still led dances like the Tsamiko, a popular dance commemorating the Greek War of Independence in 1821. In fact, my namesake, Lord Byron, supported the Greeks in their cause and is considered one of their national heroes. Nick's own colorful past included a stint in the Greek army during the Greco-Turk war of 1919-1922. His colorful demeanor and flowing white moustache made him the star of several Greek travel films in the 60's. In one film he is seen leading the tsamiko in the colorful costume of Greek Palace Guards. He told me he was once captured by the Turks during the war and he owed his life to his dancing skill. His Turkish captors were so impressed with his dancing talent, they released him. Although the Intersection is now closed, occasional reunions of its past patrons rekindles memories of Nick.

Master Teachers

During the sixties our family folk dance activities intensified. Our exposure to so many master teachers gave us a firm foundation in many of the best and most popular folk dances. My attraction to folk dancing remains keen to this day even though I have pursued other dance forms since. But we were caught up in folk dancing at a time it was at its zenith in Southern California. Europe's master teachers were defecting and many were settling in Southern California. These master performers and teachers became our heroes and mentors.

It is difficult to say which master teacher had the most influence on my family. Folk dancing covers a lot of territory and each master teacher was usually aligned with a particular county and its dances. Most of the dances we performed were line dances from Serbia, Croatia, Macedonia, Bulgaria, Romania, Greece, Turkey, Armenia and Israel. The couple dance routines were usually associated with Poland, Sweden, Hungary and Russia. Most dancers have personal preferences for music as well as teachers. They take pride in the scope of their dancing skills and the range of master teachers they have learned from.

Master Teachers

Many folk dancers could readily qualify for a master teacher designation. The regular teachers at the Intersection certainly qualified as did many leaders at the club level. I would add Donna Tripp, Beverly Barr, Vicki Maheu and Charlotte and Robin Byron to the master teacher list. Their love of the dance and precision in execution set a high standard and challenge.

The following master teachers were, for the most part, natives of the country whose dance they taught. Generally, they introduced each of their dances with an explanation of its origin, the meaning of a song's lyrics and drill on the correct pronunciation of the dance name Many of these teachers were also gifted musicians. They played instruments foreign to many Americans like the zorna (Turkish flute), gayda (Bulgarian-Serbian bagpipe), the cimbalom (Romanian strings) and the oud and bouzouki (Greek-Arabic strings). Their knowledge of music enhanced their ability to move so precisely to the various musical rhythms. Rhythms could vary from 2/4 and 4/4 to 5/8, 7/16 and 9/16. Those rhythms sounded like hat sizes to me and I was never schooled to my satisfaction in how those rhythms were categorized. I could dance to the music much easier than I could ever explain its rhythm.

Each master teacher was a personification of his native country's dance culture. Most were former national stars and considered national treasures. All were lead dancers and choreographers for major performing groups sponsored by the State. Now these European dance treasures became our own. Some of the most notable of the European stars and individuals I knew personally included:

Bora Gajicki

Bora Gajicki was one of the first master teachers that Bernie, Charlotte, Robin and I got to know pretty well. He was a star performer in his former Yugoslavian homeland. To see him perform was a thrilling experience. I have seen him make leaps in a solo performance that rivalled Barishnikov. His moves, whether dancing the Kolo, a common, handheld or belthold dance, or a more complex dance, were graceful and intricate. His timing was perfect. He was poetry in motion. He was the folk dancer equivalent to Barishnikov. Bora had some interesting stories about his old country experiences. One involved an unforgettable meeting with the Yugoslavian strong man, Marshal Tito. It seems Bora was the guest of honor at an event attended by Tito. After performing, Bora was seated next to Tito. During the course of the conversation with Tito, who was dressed in a white military uniform, Bora accidentally knocked over a glass of red wine which ended up on the Marshal's while uniform. It was an awkward moment for Bora who quickly apologized. Tito, in turn, was very gracious about the accident but that was a standout memory for Bora. Soon after the wine spilling event, Bora met Marge, an American girl and wife to be, who was travelling in Yugoslavia at the time. They were married and moved to a new home in Long Beach, California. Although Bora's exodus from Yugoslavia had nothing to do with the Tito incident, we occasionally joked that it was.

Bora was an accomplished musician and enjoyed playing the accordion. He formed a band and played at folk festivals and church events all over Southern California. I know Bora enjoyed playing as much as dancing.

Marge and Bora also had a small shop in Long Beach, the Folk Motif. Among other things, they sold folk dance clothing and opanke, the traditional leather footwear of village dancers. Many folk dancers adopted this footwear. I wore opanke for awhile but I found these flat-soled shoes tiring on my legs. I preferred a dance shoe with a heel.

We lost Bora to an injury sustained in a fall from a ladder while working at home in 2008. This untimely death was a very great loss to his family and the dancing community. But Bora left a legacy of great dances and great music. His memory always brings a smile to my face.

David Brothers

The David brothers, Mihai and Alexandru, were born in Romania and were a genuine force in popularizing Romanian dances throughout Southern California. Unlike the heavier movements of Bulgarian and

Serbian dances, Mihai's Romanian dances incorporated a lightness, grace, speed, a lot of heel stomps, the prancing motion of horses and the gliding motion of skaters. When Romanian music was played, you knew you were in for some vigorous exercise. Some of the music reflected a Gypsy influence. But heel stomping was characteristic and helped popularize the wearing of T shirts emblazoned with STAMP OUT ROMANIAN DANCING.

Mihai was tall, slender and dark haired; Alexandru was a bit shorter with piercing blue eyes. Mihai was a favorite with the girls. They were fond of his "cute tush". But everyone found his smile and sense of humor as captivating as his teaching and dancing. Like all the master teachers, he exuded self-possession and challenged his students to replicate his posture and energy. Alexandru, on the other hand, had an air of mystery about him, was more subdued than Mihai and, although an excellent Romanian line dancer, preferred the more classic couple dances of eastern Europe and Russia. Another brother, Gigi, whom I never saw dance, was an entrepreneur. He engaged in a variety of enterprises ranging from automotive repair and boat building to making slivovitz, a plum brandy, and helping his brothers run a coffee house.

Stories about Mihai and Alexandru's defection from Romania and escape from behind the iron curtain would have made a thrilling movie. Mihai was the first to defect and make it to America. Alexandru's opportunity to defect didn't arise until several years later. But the brothers had parallel careers. Even as children, they grew up studying classical ballet, character dance and modern dance. Both were lead dancers and key figures in the Romanian State Folk Ballet and Music Hall Ensemble. Both were horsemen and both even acted as stuntmen for Romanian movies. When Mihai got to America he joined the Army and accelerated his path to citizenship.

Mihai formed a Romanian dance troupe which included Charlotte as one of the performers. Bernie and I knew the parents of another girl in the troupe, Carolyn Reese. Carolyn would marry Mihai and give him a beautiful daughter. I remember meeting their daughter years later at one of Mihai's workshops in San Diego.

Mihai's dark hair is now streaked with silver but his body is still as lithe as ever and his sense of humor just as keen. Although he takes a little breather between dances, his movements are as graceful as ever. Alexandru also continues to teach more classical forms of dance including ballroom in the Los Angeles area.

Our Anaheim home had become a center for many folk dance parties. We had a large patio area, a large selection of records and convenient street parking. We also entertained many of the master teachers at our home. When the David brothers came to visit, Charlotte usually talked Mihai into playing tennis at the nearby local high school. Sooner or later, though, music prevailed and the visit would conclude with dancing.

Atanas Kolarovski

Atanas Kolarovski was and remains our leading exponent of Macedonian dances. A long time artistic director, choreographer and lead dancer for Tanec, the Macedonian State Folk Ensemble and several other groups, Atanas, like his fellow master teachers, introduced an impressive number of dances noted for their intricate rhythms. Like Bora Gajicki, Atanas played the accordion. He also played the tupan (double headed drum) and flute. His permanent home was in Seattle where he and his wife used to operate a restaurant. He enjoyed visiting us in Anaheim because he could find some relief there from the constant demands of admirers to lead or review dances He enjoyed relaxing at our home and taking his "medicine"– vodka and orange.

Mary Kobetich, a close friend and fellow folk dancer, was Macedonian and had many relatives living there. She was our original link to Atanas. Mary also helped popularize Macedonian beans at our potluck dinners. These were absolutely delicious. But I found other foods from the area, like cabbage rolls (sarma), a little bland for my taste.

Unfortunately, old country political dissensions are not always left behind. Old country dissensions and hatreds do not die easily. Animosities surface on occasion between the Greeks and the Turks, the Armenians and the Turks and within the former Yugoslavian community. At a folk dance camp at UC Santa Barbara during the early seventies a political dissension of some sort arose between Atanas and Bora. The next day, one appeared at a workshop sporting a black eye. Robin, known for her mimicking ability, characteristically imitated Bora's dance stance (arms close to his side, bent at the elbows and wrist) and would point to her eye. The dancers caught on and laughter spread. That laughter helped smooth over their differences. Bora and Atanas were friends again by the end of the day.

Robin's mimicking ability had a lot to do with her talent for replicating the styling of the masters. Her proficiency in capturing the dancing style of the masters frequently won her a prized place in the front of the line – right next to the master teacher. This was a privileged position, one usually reserved for those with superior dancing ability. Charlotte and Robin enjoyed this position in the line frequently.

Bora Ozkok

Bora Ozkok introduced Turkish folk dancing with a flair and a personality undeniably Turkish. Like some other master dancers, athletics had a dominant influence in his early school years. Swimming, soccer and wrestling were his favorite sports. He was a member of the Turkish swim team and competed in the 1960 Rome Olympics. He came to UC Berkeley by way of an athletic scholarship and majored in architecture. It was at Berkeley that Bora was introduced to folk dancing. On a return trip to Turkey, he learned the dances of his homeland from members of the Turkish National Folk Dance Ensemble. He then returned to the US to teach the dances and lead tours to Turkey.

Many of the Turkish dances possessed a unique, warrior-like vigor. A line of dancers with arms bent at the elbow and fingers interlaced would bend from the waist, bend at the knees, straighten up with bouncing movements and moving in the line of dance. The energizing music would be overshadowed by the blair of the zurna. This small, hornlike instrument, had a very distinctive sound – a cross between a blare and a shriek. That sound was so identified with the Turks that those who had suffered at their hands like the Armenians would feign disdain when they heard the instrument. Tom Bozigian, of Armenian descent and an Armenian master teacher was a good friend of Bora's but would playfully feign disdain whenever Bora would play the zurna.

Bora was always a colorful sight whether teaching or playing musical instruments. In addition to the zurna, he played the gayda, flute, drum, mandolin and several other instruments. He usually wore opanke with heavy woolen socks and sometimes a bandana around his head. He also had an uncontrolled blinking in one of his eyes. Robin picked up on this tick. If she were dancing with Bora or doing Turkish dancing elsewhere, she could distract you with her antics – like a Bora-mimicking blinking of her eyes as she led the line.

Tom Bozigian

Tom Bozigian was a master teacher of Armenian dances but unlike the other masters, Tom was born in Los Angeles. And, like Bora Ozkok, Tom was athletic. Volley ball was one of his passions and he liked handball. Tom and I never managed to meet on a handball court although we challenged each other to a match every time we met.

Like the David's, Tom studied both ballet and Armenian dance in Armenia. On an invite from then Soviet Armenia, he studied at the State Choreographic School. His dancing studies in Armenia included classical, Russian character and Armenian. I took several Armenian dance classes from Tom. The little pinky hold used in the line dances was distinctly Armenian. Tom was also a very talented musician. His finger dexterity on the doumbec (stemmed drum) could almost make that instrument talk.

The sixties put folk dancing on the map in Southern California. It was an exciting time; a decade that popularized folk dancing in Southern California, attracted an impressive array of world class teachers and established the Intersection as the focal point for folk dance enthusiasts throughout the southland.

The influence of the master teachers in the sixties stimulated the growth of an enthusiastic and expanding group of folk dancers especially in Southern California. Many were travelling to Balkan states, learning new dances firsthand and teaching them upon return. Several were forming exhibition groups of their own. These individuals would be assuming leadership positions in the clubs and would be prized for their introduction of new dances.

Any roster of respected dancers, in addition to the master teachers, would include Billy Burke, Dick Oakes, Barry Glass, Paul Sheldon and, of course, Athan Karras. Beverly Barr, Vikki Maheu, Mikki Revenaugh, Donna Tripp and Sunni Bloland would also grace the list as folk dance standouts. If we had a Folk Dancers Hall of Fame, all of these individuals should be included. But of all the dancers I've known, I never met anyone who could match the range of folk dances that Vikki Maheu knew and could teach. Dick Oakes was in the same category.

There are, of course, many other highly regarded dancers not mentioned here. For this I apologize and attribute it to a faulty memory.

Chapter 5

The SEVENTIES

Standout events of the seventies include the Mylai Massacre, the Pentagon Papers, the right to vote for 18 year olds, Nixon's visit to China, Watergate, Vietnam cease-fire, the energy crisis, the Nixon resignation, oil company profits, a US unemployment rate of over 9%, the death of Howard Hughes and Elvis Presley, Jonestown, Jimmy Carter's election, diplomatic relations with China and the exile of the Shah of Iran.

The Urban Systems Institute

Neil Armstrong put his footprint on the moon on 20 July 1969. "One small step for man; one giant leap for mankind." But once that goal was achieved, the aerospace industry began winding down. Vietnam had become a funding priority at the expense of the space programs. As the emphasis on space programs diminished, many engineers and other aerospace workers in Southern California were finding themselves in unemployment lines and getting their first taste of economic hardship. The unemployment rate was soaring.

With my working experience in both aerospace and local government, I couldn't respond fast enough to a call from the County's Comprehensive Area Manpower Planning Commission. It was a call for proposals to get people back to work. Orange County's unemployment rate at the time was over ten percent. Engineers and other professionals, long accustomed to job security, now found themselves among the ranks of the unemployed, an unthinkable position just two years earlier. Vietnam was unpopular and NASA was vulnerable now that the lunar landing was accomplished. The aerospace industry in Southern California was hit hard, especially Orange County. The Manpower Planning Commission was trying to move at flank speed to get the unemployed back on payrolls. A special allocation of several million dollars from the Department of Labor was made available to counties for programs that could prepare the unemployed for jobs in new areas. It was a competitive process geared primarily to those operating at a vocational rather than professional level. But the aerospace downsizing had filled the unemployment lines with an unusually high number of professionals.

I proposed a training center that would prepare unemployed professionals for new careers in government. The program would be a combination of class work and field work. The field work would consist of completing priority tasks that local governments wanted done. Having worked in Anaheim's city hall manager's office, I knew many of the city administrators in the county. This facilitated the collaboration needed to get their endorsement and willingness to promote the employment of these professionals in the public sector. I was among several selected to received federal funding under a special program for training the unemployed for jobs in sectors that would be hiring. I developed a training curriculum, established a budget, recruited a training staff, secured the sponsorship of participating public agencies and called the program the "Civic-Oriented Manpower Utilization Program". The California State Department of Education would have program oversight. I then proceeded to recruit forty candidates by making the rounds of several Employment Centers where, with support from Experience Unlimited, an engineering self-help group, was able to provide an orientation that would help channel the right people into the program. I was seeking a mix of engineers and administrators, college-educated for the most part, who would be part of multi-disciplined teams working to solve real problems confronting local governments. I made the point that they would be working at a level and in a style comparable to their aerospace days.

During contractor orientations, I remember being approached by the director of a program geared primarily to lesser skilled workers.

"You know, Bob, your job is much harder than mine. My people are used to being on and off payrolls and scraping by. They know the drill. But your engineers and professionals are going through this for the first time. It's harder on them." I knew exactly what he meant.

Before the money came in, I was able to jump start the program into motion by securing a classroom on a high school campus in Westminster. The Garden Grove Unified School District was supportive of our program and I was able to conduct the program under Adult Education pending receipt of federal funds.

The program began with a classroom orientation in local government organization, financial systems and the political context. I invited managers of different city and county departments to come before the class to describe their roles, typical problems, the public sector environment and the attitudes they might encounter. A manager from the County Human Resource department let the participants know that not everyone was happy with using government as a job source for former aerospace engineers.

"There is a certain resentment among some public employees who look on your entry to public service as a harbor of last resort. They feel that you have been enjoying the good life and high salaries in the private sector and now want the security of a public service job."

Although not exactly what I had in mind when I invited public managers to participate in our program, it was something that had to be said. True, these former aerospace professionals did enjoy high salaries, good benefits, and great housing in high-priced areas. Some had boats with docking facilities. But now these aerospace engineers were seeing their living standards crumble before their eyes. Boats had to be sold, club memberships would lapsed, subscriptions had to be cancelled and eating out was becoming a rare event. Marriages were strained, divorce was not uncommon and, in one instance, there was a suicide.

The high school campus environment came along just in time. It was a real tonic for the participants. Between the pledge of allegiance and loudspeaker interruptions announcing sporting events and high school dances, the upbeat campus atmosphere and the contagion of youthful enthusiasm had a revitalizing effect on our participants. One of our program participants even had a son on campus in his senior year. The faculty lounge with its fresh coffee and doughnuts was available to our entire class. Training allowances in lieu of unemployment checks were now being mailed to participants eliminating the need for visits to the Employment Office for check pick-up. With the federal money now coming in, we bid farewell to the high school and moved into rented facilities on the UC Irvine campus.

Our new quarters were on the second floor of a UC Irvine bookstore, restaurant and Post Office. We purchased classroom equipment – chairs, tables, white boards etc. We held classes three days a week, mostly in the morning. The rest of the time was spent on tackling tasks the local governments had assigned. Each participating agency had specific problems they wanted solved and were relying on our skill as objective professionals to move them forward in areas where they lacked the in-house expertise. Our teams usually consisted of four individuals, each with education or experience related to the problem at hand. With forty participants we had as many as ten teams in motion most of the time, each team assigned to a different agency and each team working on a different assignment.

The academic level and work experience of our participants rivaled that of the top consulting firms in the country. We were identified as the Urban Systems Institute and counted among our trainee college majors electrical engineering, mechanical engineering, physics, chemistry, math, accounting and business administration. Several had master's and one had a Ph.D. Their prior work affiliations included General Dynamics, Ford Aeronautical, Lockheed, Grumman, Hughes, McDonnell, Douglas, TRW, Rockwell and Northrop.

The tasks assigned by local agencies covered a variety of challenging assignments. These included reconfiguring and integrating radio communications for city and the county law enforcement, improving drug-related information exchange among law enforcement agencies, recommending new surfacing materials for streets, streamlining admission procedures at the County hospital, improving procurement practices at Santa Ana Community College, developing an entirely new organizational structure for Orange County, determining the impact of socio-economics on student progress for the Garden Grove school district, and developing maintenance schedules for Anaheim Union High.

When a study was completed, it was presented to the requesting agency in both oral and written form but not before each team's study findings were reviewed before the Institute as a whole. This meant that everyone in the training program could volunteer critiques or suggestions for improving the presentation. This interchange was the key to our success. The professional level of the work was so pronounced that major consulting firms already on contract with County agencies began complaining that our free work was cutting into their business.

At one point, I was approached by a major consulting firm and asked if I would be willing to sell the enterprise. At the time, I said no. But looking back, the wiser choice might have been a yes.

My biggest misgiving with the program's outcome was not convincing the public agencies to keep our study teams intact. Our team members would lose their effectiveness if hired on a solo basis. Yet that was the traditional way of measuring a program's success. But if hired individually, they would have been smothered in the bureaucracy. I felt then and still do that the teams we deployed would have provided a better service had they remained intact. The individuals in our program were effective because they worked as teams. Their identity as staff members of the Urban Systems Institute gave them a sense of identity comparable to their relationship with their former employers.

A few weeks before the program drew to a close, I hosted a luncheon for city officials during which I proposed transitioning our organization to a consulting firm status. Members would continue to solve problems just as before only, this time, study results could be shared with all government entities within Orange County. To finance the operation, we suggested annual dues from participating local governments and grants from foundations and government agencies. Although the concept did not gain traction at the time, I believe the concept of using professional talent productively remains as viable today as it was then. I think thousands of talented individuals could be employed today on infrastructure upgrades and digital system streamlines.

I spent a few weeks winding down the program and storing the equipment. For awhile I rented a Newport Beach motel room where I worked uninterruptedly on follow-on proposals. The only ones who knew where I was at the time were my wife and my secretary. The walls of that motel room were plastered with outlines of follow-on proposals. When I emerged, I put together a UCI college radio talk show program that engaged professionals in discussions related to product development in the local high tech industry.

At this time, I also developed a proposal for a US Academy of Education. This Academy would develop master educators who would review the teaching methods used by the most effective schools both at home and abroad while publicizing the results in report form and at conferences. We presented the concept to UCI students. However, the Vietnam experience was a sour one and any word smacking of militarism turned them off. The world "Academy" stirred a mental connection to West Point and Annapolis. It turned them off. The concept was put aside for another day.

Another proposal involved acquiring a converted Navy minesweeper of WWII vintage, traveling to foreign ports to review and developing documentaries featuring methods used by foreign port operators to meet both port needs and the needs of the adjacent communities. These documentaries would be transmitted to Public Administration centers across the US. Although the concept was not broadly publicized, a number of academics expressed a willing to participate. We even surveyed the boat market for a converted Navy minesweeper similar to one John Wayne owned and had docked at Newport Beach. We even had a qualified boat captain ready to go. Unfortunately, we didn't nail the funds.

Small Business

After a much needed family vacation in Ensenada, I found myself pounding the pavement for a new contract or job. I had a temporary respite as a Project Director for a small business development program for minority entrepreneurs. The program was designed to demonstrate the effectiveness of a small business training center for minority entrepreneurs. The program's effectiveness would be measured in terms of approved business loans from local banks or banks with Small Business Administration loan guarantees. We had only six months to demonstrate the validity of the program after which we were to morph into a larger program. With a small staff, we were able to put together a concentrated course on how to make a business plan. We put several applicants for our service through the course. But to ensure the viability the business plans or loan packages, we developed a community review board. This board consisted of local representatives from banking, legal, accounting, insurance and local government. We would present our loan packages to the board and incorporate their suggestions for strengthening the package. This expedited the loan granting process and helped a couple new businesses get off the ground.

Charlotte on Canyon High Tennis Team, Anaheim Hills, 1976

Administrative staffers learning operating
basics of high tech products.

The roundtable approach has been my modus operandi ever since my General Dynamics days. Calling together community members whose services are vital to the success of a small business community was a winning formula. Soon after completing this project, I expanded this approach by opening the program to the community at large under the auspices of Santa Ana Community College. This was a very popular program and drew large audiences. We were partnered with the Small Business Administration and professionals from primary support groups such as accounting, legal, marketing, banking, insurance, licensing and regulatory bodies. Our presentation facilities were always filled to capacity.

Gymkhana

About this time, I developed a program called "Gymkhama". This program provided a joint parent-student learning experience over a series of Saturday mornings on the Santa Ana College campus. It blended a physical activity with a companion academic subject. The physical activities included gymnastics, martial arts, folk dancing and scuba. The academics included science, physics, history and music. Principles of science and physics were related to Scuba, martial arts and gymnastics. History and music were related to folk dancing. A special interdisciplinary team was organized for this program. The program targeted middle school age children and their parents. My fix on children of middle school age would later emerge as a target group for a charter school

During the 70's, the political scene was in turmoil given the Watergate break-in and the subsequent resignation of Nixon. It was also a time of personal turmoil as the behavior of Ginny and Mark began putting a real strain on my family and marital relations.

Mark's Epilepsy

Mark's behavior was affecting relationships at home and at school. His coterie of friends was small and they were not the best influences. Mark's classroom behavior resulted in my meeting with the school's vice-principal on a couple of occasions but the desired results were not being reflected in Mark's performance. He was on dilantin for seizure suppression and, if he missed taking it, there was the possibility of a seizure. We could recognize when a seizure was coming by his slurred speech. Mark seemed to recognize this seizure warning sign and would stay close to home around this time. We could help him when a seizure did occur at home. I think Mark was aware of his seizure episodes and wanted to keep them out of public view.

A stress-free environment is recommended for epileptics as is doing what you like and are good at. Regular high school was not a good environment for Mark. He got a job working with his hands, making boats and surfboards, something he liked and a popular industry in the Santa Ana-Newport Beach area. Mark was eighteen now and dropped out of school. He never received a regular high school diploma although he may have completed a GED.

Mark's self-sustaining career was launched. It would be in construction with occasional odd jobs related to scuba diving, boat maintenance and sea urchin harvesting. These were things he liked to do and could do well. It went back to the very things he liked as a little tike – hammering and swimming.

We kept Mark's room open for him to use whenever he wanted but Mark was showing an independent streak. He was showing us he could make it on his own. He was not going to let his affliction stand in the way. He even got his own car – a VW wagon and Mark never seemed to want for a girl friend.

Ginny's Schizophrenia

Ginny, on the other hand, had already graduated from Villa Park High and was working as a receptionist and cashier at Bob's Big Boy in Santa Ana. But her moods and paranoia became more apparent after she took up with some fundamentalist Christian sect in Santa Ana. She also bought a car – a used Chevy that she thought she could keep in good mechanical condition by praying. She developed a fetish for cleanliness using alcohol wipes on the phone mouthpiece every time she finished using it. And, there were times when she would let loose with a stream of four letter words. She was hearing voices and spoke about an outside network that was sending messages to her brain.

It was like pulling teeth to get Ginny to see the County psychiatrist. We were distressed about her condition. She had medication she wouldn't take. She continued talking to herself and responding to imaginary voices. We were able to get her committed one weekend at a county facility. There, they made sure she took her medications. When she returned, she had the appearance of normalcy for a few days. But it wasn't long before her characteristic behavior returned. She wouldn't take her medication.

She signed up with a temporary agency and worked on and off as office help. The short term assignments seemed to work because Ginny could convey a sense of normalcy over a brief period. But the chinks in her armor would appear anytime she spent more than a couple days with the same employer. It wouldn't be long before Ginny would be living on the street, phoning me on occasion to say she was alright or arranging to meet with me for lunch. She usually called from out of town. Santa Monica was her favorite haunt. She wore a hooded sweat shirt that hid her face. She feared being committed or confined. She would never sign anything – like an application for disability and housing assist. It was heartbreaking. The mental health people and social workers told me there was not much I could do as long as she posed no threat to herself or others. Ginny refused to take advantage of the several shelters available for women. The most I could do for Ginny was to bring her fresh clothes and a few dollars.

I have been so frustrated with the lack of support or care for the mentally ill.. At the time, the big push was for getting the mentally ill out of institutionalized settings and back into a home environment and normal societal associations. There is nothing more difficult to manage than mental illness. I don't know how many families are just torn apart in attempts to manage the care of a loved one afflicted with a mental disorder. I don't know where common sense has gone in this country. We seem to be more hung up on protecting the rights of mentally incompetent to the neglect of their health and return to normalcy. Stray dogs get better care.

Charlotte and Robin

Charlotte and Robin were doing well at the new Canyon High School located right behind our home in Anaheim. Both graduated from there.

Charlotte was an excellent student, a member of the tennis team and a leader of many school activities. In recognition of her academic and leadership abilities, she was inducted into the school district's special category of students identified as the Top Forty, an exclusive society for the district's best, all-round student leaders.

Robin was also a good student and a star member of the girls' track team. She drew much of her running motivation from her track coach. She was a real standout when it came to running marathons. I admired Robin's guts and stamina for competing in that grueling 26.2 mile run. As much as I was into jogging and physical conditioning, the marathon was only a dream in my book.

At this point in our marriage, dancing was the glue holding the family together We were travelling to the Intersection at least once a week, taking weekly classes from Billy Burke or Barry Glass at the Hollywood Playground and Romanian classes from Mihai David at a coffee house on Sunset Blvd. Whenever Billy or Barry were unable to teach, Charlotte or Robin would take over. In addition to Aman tours, Charlotte was also performing as a member of Mihai's Romanian dance troupe. Dancing was a major part of our lives.

Senior Citizens

The 70's were also an era when government resources were focused on the senior community. City halls were operating activity centers for seniors where nutritious meals were being served at minimal cost. Activities stimulating the mind and body were provided. Adult schools helped enriched these centers with academics, crafts and exercise programs. I began teaching World Affairs for Garden Grove Adult and soon made that program one of the largest in the area. At the same time, I extended the class into other parts of the community as an adjunct faculty member for Santa Ana and Fullerton community colleges. Later, I expanded the same program into Whittier, Norwalk and La Mirada. I was holding classes in ten different facilities each week. My student enrollment was over 300.

I enjoyed the off-campus freedom and the stimulation of meeting with so many different groups. The classes were usually held in comfortable living rooms or dining areas. I blended the culture, music and dance of foreign places around an academic core of presentations and discussions of World Affairs. I also used film to reinforce our discussions. Participants were usually well read and enjoyed keeping abreast of the world around them. They prized the mental stimulation and the social interaction. One of the participants, wheel chair bound, was stimulated enough to run for seat on the local Water Board. Although he didn't win, his actions made him a celebrity among his fellow residents. They also enjoyed the music and dance demonstrations. And, periodically, I would have students from local high schools bused to my off-site locations for cross generational sessions. The exchange of views between the young and the old was a positive experience for all. By now, the program format had gelled into one comparable to a television show. I was integrating lecture, discussion, film, music, dance, cross-generational experiences and guest appearances.

Pendleton Revisited

About this time, Camp Pendleton was being used as a processing center for refugees from the Vietnam war. Most were South Vietnamese but there were Cambodians, Loatians, and Hmong as well. I visited this multi-lingual staging area where the refugees were being processed and assigned to more permanent locations throughout the country. It wasn't long before cities like Garden Grove would reflect the presence of these new refugee groups. Native style restaurants, food outlets and small businesses would pop up wherever they settled. With advertising and businesses being promoted in their own language, sections of a city took on the semblance of an Asian market place.

While at Camp Pendleton, I felt like a roving reporter. I would take my eye-witness experience back to my students. Visiting the base brought back memories of my own earlier service in the Corps and new possibilities for the senior community. It got me thinking about developing a program that might condition seniors for more active roles in the community. This would entail recruiting relatively able bodied seniors who might benefit from the physical and mental stimulus of reliving their youth as members of the Armed Services. A platoon-sized group of retirees would be uniformed, live in tents or barracks and go through a modified Marine workday for 30-90 days. The daily regiment would include moderate exercises, studies of US and Marine Corps history, training in first aid and emergency operations, eating in a mess hall and having liberty on week-ends. It was my belief that letting seniors relive the experience of their youth would be a tonic for body and spirit and could be of practical value to the community. After their conditioning, the retirees would be ready for community work for as long as they chose. I talked it up with more active seniors and several were willing to participate. I wrote to the Marine Commandant for possible use of a small segment of the base. He referred me to the Base Commander. That's where it stopped. I never followed thru. But the concept lingers I recently suggested that former Marines might provide administrative or civil affairs support to Marine overseas operations.

Educational Service Corps

I then put together a new non-profit corporation, the Educational Service Corps. This non-profit was designed to engage my most active seniors as directors on a real corporation organized for educational purposes. One of the proposals I developed for the new non-profit involved the formation of an expeditionary corps of teachers who would travel the world updating existing documentaries on foreign countries and creating new ones where none existed. Too many films in our schools and film libraries were out of date. Although we did not attract any funding, we did attract material support. From organizations like Hughes Aircraft and Disneyland, we received desks, chairs, file cabinets, publication support and even television production support.

But in June 1978, Prop 13 came along. That voter initiative put a cap on property taxes. This had a dampening effect on many educational programs. The easy expansion of adult classes of the early seventies slowed considerably; many disappeared.

Saturday Night Fever

Meanwhile, a new dance craze was making its mark - Disco. This was a smooth couple dance popularized by John Travolta in Saturday Night Fever. This film kicked off a new dancing craze across the country. Night clubs in the Disneyland vicinity were taken up with the dance. Some were offering free dance lessons. I couldn't resist and began taking lessons. I tried to get Bernie involved but she was entrenched in folk dancing and her folk dance friends. The night club scene didn't appeal to her nor did the bar atmosphere. As for the bar environment, it never got to me. My interest was in the dance and I liked the music.

The dance uniform of the day for disco was business casual – suit or vest and tie optional. The women usually wore a cocktail dress and high heels. But disco was one of the most short lived dance styles I ever experienced. The dance peaked in less than two years. It was gone as suddenly as it appeared. But like other dances that matched the music of the day, its moves would transition into other dances like the Hustle and West Coast Swing.

The seventies ended on an uncertain note. Prop 13 was cutting into the expansion of senior programs. My teaching was gravitating towards school–business partnerships, technology expositions and programs of a cross-generational nature. Meanwhile, my marriage was feeling the strain of Ginny and Mark's condition and the stress of a fluctuating income.

Chapter 6

The EIGHTIES

Highlights of the eighties included the Carter boycott of the 1980 summer Olympics in Moscow, Ronald Reagan's election, Japan's ascendancy as a premiere automaker, the failed rescue of hostages in Iran, the first launch of space shuttle Columbia,the release of US hostages from Iran, Michael Jackson's Thriller, the Falklands, Grenada, the LA summer Olympics,the Challenger explosion, the Chernobyl nuclear disaster, the Iran-Contra scandal and the departure of the Soviets from Afghanistan.

School-Business Partnerships

The Educational Service Corps was still a viable 501 (c) 3 non-profit. It had already attracted donations of office furnishings from Hughes Aircraft and publication services from Disneyland. Now it was time to implement its educational mission. Our first target was non-technical employees of high tech companies. Too many of the non-engineering or non-technical staff of high tech companies had little if any knowledge about a company's high tech products. It was management's feeling that a better informed employee was more productive and more in tune with company objectives. Given the technical sophistication of the products being manufactured and developed, an invisible dividing line seemed to exist between technical and non-technical functions within a company. To erase this divide and enhance teamwork, I developed a series of educational forums at which company engineers and technical staff would provide explanations about a product's workings in terms a layman could understand.

After the first session, I learned a big lesson. It was a mistake to take engineers at their word when it came to their assertion that they could explainr high tech in plain English. I saw too many eyes glaze over during the first presentation as engineers lapsed back into the language of their peers. Thereafter, engineers would rehearse their presentations to ensure that technical terminology was reduced to language a fifth grader or adult with limited technology exposure could readily understand. We had engineers use common household items like faucets, garden hoses and electrical outlets for comparisons when describing technical functions.. The rehearsals paid off. Future presentations were much more effective.

We also provided samples of products whenever possible. Printed circuit boards and silicon wafers with imbedded microchips were popular handouts. Lasers, fiber optics and satellite dishes were among the demonstrations. There were also factory walk-throughs to view the actual manufacture of microchips. The process of photographing electrical schematics and overlaying the film on a silicon substrate then infusing gases to create microscopic gateways were technological marvels. The walk-through gave participants a much better appreciation of a product, especially the manufacture of microchips. CEOs appreciated an informed workforce more than anyone. After a series of successful employee presentations, we took our program to high school campuses.

High school principals were very receptive to the program. They endorsed our mission to motivate students to become more involved with science, math and physics. They saw the value of demonstrating high tech products, so many of which were being manufactured so close to home. Several high schools participated including Canyon High in Anaheim where my daughters were going to school. Lasers, infra-red devices, fiber optics, satellites, microchips and advanced communications were among the items used to demonstrate principles of physics, chemistry and engineering/ The turn-out on the part of students already hooked on science and math was high. For them, this was frosting on the cake and reinforced their interest in technology.

One memorable presentation took place at the El Toro Marine Airbase. The Marines at this base stood in sharp contrast to the casualness of a high school campus. The entire base had an air of discipline about it. Our target audience was the maintenance crews for the jets and helicopters. Our presentation featured a target acquisition system called FLIR, an acronym for "forward looking infra-red". This was an advanced target acquisition system. The presenters were the very engineers from nearby companies who were involved with the design of the system. The Marines were alert, had questions and took notes. It brought back memories of my own training days in Basic School at Quantico, Virginia.

These technology expos led to another opportunity to expand our presentation of high tech progress via cable television. Cable facilities and equipment were being made available on a limited basis to community non-profits for public service programs. The high tech programs we were presenting in convention centers and high school campuses fit the bill. After conferring with the engineers participating in our program, the navigational satellites then being built by Rockwell at Seal Beach were selected for presentation. The Cable studios located on the Chapman College campus in the city of Orange would host the event.

Since our knowledge of operating television studio equipment was non-existent, we turned to Hughes Aircraft in Fullerton for help. Hughes very generously donated the time and professional know-how of their TV production staff. We were off and running.

Putting together a TV special is exciting. There's a lot of planning, organizing, scheduling, rehearsal, selection of props and even the selection of background music. I was partial to the tune of Around the World in Eighty Days but we ended up using music from Star Wars. We were fortunate to have the very engineers currently engaged in satellite design, geosynchronous orbits, antennas and launching systems as our presenters. The props we used were either the real thing or realistic models. Our final product was an hour long educational TV program with language geared to a lay audience.

I used my copy of the Satellite tape to introduce my adult and high school students to the new navigational marvels. But the primary beneficiary of these technology expositions was myself. I had to make sure that the technology explanations were suited to a lay audience. This was a throwback to my earlier days of technology reporting at the

Aerospace Corporation. It helped in converting high tech jargon into more readily grasped, non-technical terminology for lay audiences. Language simplification breaks down so many barriers to learning.

Computers for Kids

In the late seventies and early eighties the personal computer was making its presence known especially on school campuses. Apple II was a dominating presence on campuses and community colleges were responding to the need for orientation. One of the orientation programs was designed specifically for kids. This Computer for Kids program was quite popular. Kids took to it with enthusiasm. Computer shops and distributors were more than willing to check out computers on a free loan basis to enhance their product exposure. So whenever additional hardware was required, local vendors would come through. I also expanded the program to include adults. This marked the early stage of a technology boom that has changed the world.

Travolta Again

With the eighties came the emergence of a new dance craze. The country two-step was finding its way into bars and dance halls across the nation thanks to John Travolta and the movie hit Urban Cowboy. It seemed every engineer in Orange County was doffing his daytime business attire for nighttime western wear. Levis, boots, western style shirts and cowboy hats were the uniform of the night. The two-step was as easy as pie to learn – step together, walk, walk or slow, slow, quick, quick, slow. And western music itself had always been popular especially in the west.

One of Orange County largest and most popular dance hall was the Cowboy, located just a couple blocks from Disneyland and Anaheim's commercial hub of Harbor and Katella. Jack Wade, the owner, knew how to run a dance hall. The Cowboy featured three dance floors- a main one and two smaller ones. . Admission was free if you got there early or had an easy to come by pass. There was also a Happy Hour where the free buffet was substantial enough for a regular meal. Dance instruction took place nightly right after the Happy Hour. Following the dance lesson, music and dance would be non-stop well after midnight.

The parking lot also served as a headquarters for many a romantic tryst. You couldn't find a friendlier place.

I took Bernie there once and that was it for her. She didn't like the environment and she wasn't impressed by the people she met there. Our dancing relationship was growing apart and uncivil tones were creeping into our conversations. I was gone a lot. Bernie wasn't happy. Except for folk dancing, we were doing less and less together. Ginny and Mark added to the strain. Ginny's schizophrenia was becoming more pronounced. She was still hearing voices, talking to herself and not taking her medicine. It was a time when California's mental health care was being cut back to the bare bones. Unfortunately, treatment of the mentally ill is a sad chapter in California's history. Even today it is estimated that about half the homeless are suffering from some sort of mental disorders.

Mark and Macho Sports

Mark was still having his occasional seizures although he was much better than Ginny when it came to taking his medicine. His circle of friends remained limited and he had dropped out of school. But he was good with his hands and was able to support himself doing construction work and building boats and surfboards. He enjoyed hammering things since he was a little boy. And, when I outfitted him a scuba gear for Christmas, Mark turned to the ocean as his primary source of recreation. His swimming skills paid off. Few knew California's underwater coastline better than Mark. From the La Jolla trench off of Scripps to Moss Street in Laguna, to Catalina and the Channel Isles, few could match his knowledge of these dive waters. But he usually broke the cardinal rule of SCUBA diving – not to dive alone. Unless Mark was off on a boat dive, he generally dove alone. I often worried about the possibility of an underwater seizure but it never happened.

Mark was also involved with the martial arts and would invite me to his tournaments. Then he got into parachute jumping. I remember him telling me that on his first jump, his main chute wouldn't open and he had to use the emergency chute. That didn't cool his ardor for jumping at all. Later when he was working on the oil company spill responder ship, he started taking helicopter flying lessons until the cost scotched that ambition. In all the things he undertook including shooting, scuba, martial arts, and parachuting, he excelled.

One of Mark's best friends was Frank a former Marine whose hobbies coincided with his - scuba diving and shooting. When Frank moved from San Diego to Florida to work for a defense contractor, they would exchange visits. When in Florida, Mark and Frank would dive some of the Caribbean Islands. Frank was a licensed pilot and together they would fly to favorite dive spots. In fact, Charlotte, also a certified diver, joined Mark on at least one occasion to dive a favorite Caribbean spot before she married.

Charlotte and Robin

Our youngest girls continued to do well. Charlotte was going to Cal State Fullerton and doing well. She would also tackle some automotive problems that were generally reserved for older boys or mechanics – liking replacing a car's water pump. When her pump went out, Charlotte balked at the labor charge for replacing the pump and did it herself. I always thought that was pretty gutsy.

Meantime, Robin was about to get married. Unfortunately, the friction between Bernie and myself had rubbed off on the girls. They sided with their mother. Bernie and I were no longer sleeping together and most of our conversations were ending up in arguments. Sometimes our arguments would carry over to the kids. On one occasion we had exchanged some angry words and whether or not I would be coming to her wedding. That did it. Robin struck me off the wedding list and Bernie gave her away. She married a high school sweetheart, Steve McCamey. Steve's father, a retired Marine colonel, arranged for the wedding and reception to take place at the El Toro Marine Air Station.

Then it happened. While working out of a temporary office in Garden Grove, someone knocked on my office door and handed me an envelope. I was served the divorce papers. I did not expect this even though our loving feelings had ended some time ago. I was just resigned to a loveless or sexless marriage but never contemplated divorce. I saw nothing but an economic disaster looming. Only the lawyers would win. I felt betrayed. I had to move out of my house.

The divorce was a long time in the making. Looking back, I can see so many areas where I was at fault. My work and ambitions limited our time together. Our sex life was not the greatest. I was not big on foreplay. Most times, I was the only one satisfied. I felt unwanted. Dancing had become a sexual sublimation. On two occasions, it amounted to more than a sublimation. It did, however, take the edge off and, for awhile, made me more content at home. But I was also drinking more at home, something Charlotte and Robin noticed even more than I.

With divorce papers served and a deadline for getting out of the home, I had no idea where to live until one of my dancing friends at the Cowboy came to the rescue.

Maria

Maria was an excellent dancer, about twenty years my junior, petite and pretty. She was born in Cuba but left the island with relatives soon after Castro came to power. I met her at the Cowboy where she was a regular part of the clique I was associating with. She was not only an excellent dancer but very funny. I remember my first brush with her humor when she looked at me and said "Hi, sailor. Do you fool around on the first date?" That cracked me up. Not many girls were that forward. I wasn't used to remarks like that especially on the folk dance scene. She had a few other choice expressions but her dancing ability, size, good looks and salty language attracted me. Now that my marriage was on the rocks I started looking at Maria as a woman as much as a dance partner. Her appearance belied her actual age. I could have taken her for a teenager or someone just turning 21. But her hips and thighs were testaments to her full-fledged womanhood. When I told her about my pending divorce and how I was barred from my house, she invited me to share her apartment in East County area. Maria was divorced and had a daughter who lived with the father in an Orange County beach community. She had visiting rights on weekends once or twice a month. I moved in. My sexual drought was over.

121

Meantime my teaching continued and even expanded to include business classes at a private college and some substitute teaching in the Los Angeles area. One of those experiences took me into a high school in the East LA area close to where Jaime Escalante had such great results in teaching calculus to Latinos. The movie, "Stand and Deliver", gives an excellent portrayal of Escalante's work with his students.

General Dynamics Again

In response to one of the many resumes I had sent to companies in the San Diego area, I received a call from General Dynamics. I was asked to come in for an interview. I went, was interviewed and was hired. This would be my third time working for General Dynamics. Maria said she wanted to go with me. When I told Bernie she told me she really didn't want a divorce and that the divorce papers were intended to get me to pay more attention to her. It was another decision fork in the road. I took Maria.

General Dynamics put me up for a couple weeks at the Pacific Beach Oakwood apartments until we could find our own apartment. While at the company-funded apartment, Charlotte paid me a visit and told me all about her unique nursing internship program at the Los Angeles General Hospital. Charlotte lived at the hospital while she was interning and taking classes. I really had to hand it to Charlotte. She accomplished so much with so little help from me. She took to Maria partly because they were close in age and also because of Maria's sense of humor. I think Charlotte liked the idea I was getting a little enjoyment in life again although her first allegiance was to her mother. I understood this.

Being back with General Dynamics was like old times. Many of the people I worked with before were still there including Nellie, the department secretary. I last saw her twenty years ago yet she said hello and helped me settle in as if I had never left. I knew my new boss, Herb Richmond, from years past as well as Bob Bacon, a General Dynamics icon who knew more about Convair's history and procedures than anyone I knew. I would be doing essentially the same work as before - management and information systems. The major difference now was the product line. Before, it was the F102 and the Atlas missile. Now it would be the Cruise missile.

Meantime, Maria found a job doing what she was doing in Orange County – bank telling. It wasn't long, however, before our dancing resumed. We started a company-sponsored country two step class at General Dynamics. The turn-out was impressive. The local dance scene, however, was not as vibrant as Jack Wade's Cowboy in Orange County. But the number of smaller country western bars in East County in smaller cities bordering San Diego like Santee, El Cajon and Poway made up for it. The frequency of our dancing soon put us in the center of the dancing crowd. Not long after, we added another dimension to our dancing – clogging.

Clogging

Like square dancing, you entered the world of clogging with an introductory course before you could fit in with more experienced cloggers. A popular site for clogging was a large auditorium in Balboa Park. Cloggers shared the site with square dancers. Later, the city would convert this site into an automotive museum much to the chagrin of the dancers. But unlike the main dance ballroom in Balboa Park which was wooden, the floor of this auditorium was tile. This was hard on the legs. It was also easy to slip on which I did more than once. But people were leery of cloggers on wooden floors. They feared the metal taps on toes and heels would eat up the floor.

I don't recall what turned us on to clogging. It may have been some of our two-step friends or a flyer announcing a new clogging class. Like many dance enthusiasts, we seemed to have a built-in radar for anything that is dance-related. We brought clogging shoes and metal taps for our toes and heels. That's all we needed. The fun, of course, was tapping in time with the music. There were two types of toe taps. One was a single cleat. The other was a double cleat that would flap when dancing creating a double tapping sound. There were only two popular dance shoe colors-white and black..

Once you are part of the clogging circle, there is no end to the steps and dances you'll learn. You get to know the callers and, just like square dance callers, some are more popular than others. Our two favorite callers were Melinda Leatherman and Shirley. Our favorite dance sites were both in El Cajon: - one at the union hall on Chambers Street; the other at the Silver Spur on Main Street.

Clogging music is happy and fast. It includes bluegrass, country, rock and hip hop. The banjo and fiddle are the center piece instruments. It's a slice of Americana, tracing its early origins to Scotland and Ireland then to colonial America especially the Appalachian region. Kentucky, Tennessee, West Virginia, Virginia and North Carolina are traditionally associated with clogging. States like Kentucky and North Carolina even have clogging designated as the official State dance.

Melinda and Shirley took us through the paces and made sure we were up to the latest clogging movements and calls. Like square dancing, clogging was danced with the aid of callers. Throughout the music, dancers were continuously responding to the caller's direction. Over the clatter of the taps, you would hear calls like basic, triple, push off, double rock, clog over, stomp double, Samantha, Kentucky Drag, Cowboy, slur and Charleston. Maria was a fast learner and a standout clogger. She was invited to join a couple performing groups. But she had her own career ambitions and was determined not to let any grass grow under her feet. At my urging, she acquired citizenship and graduated from a local university.

I had affectionately dubbed Maria "Pumpkin", a name used exclusively by me. We had more than our share dancing on both the two-step and clogging scene. Maria also enjoyed her frequent visits to her daughter. I had held on to one of my Saturday classes even after I moved to San Diego. The Orange County beach area was nearby so while I was teaching a World Affairs class, Maria was able to pick up her daughter and we could all return to San Diego together. We would also have to return Jennifer and this meant a couple round trips on weekends until her daughter was old enough and comfortable enough to ride the train on her own.

Maria was working part time at a local bank when she got a grant from a local San Diego foundation as an award for her scholastic achievements at San Diego State. She decided to use the money to attend paralegal training in Arizona. That's when our relationship began falling apart. We were now living in a new apartment complex in Del Mar Heights after living at a Pacific Beach apartment for about 4 years. But when Maria returned from her training in Arizona, she seemed to have done some reflecting on our relationship. She was forcing my hand. I had been avoiding the marriage issue from the beginning. She would now say to me "How come I am good enough to live with but not good enough to marry?" It was a question I knew would come sooner or later. Our relationship was cooling. My primary reluctance to marriage was our age difference. It was only a matter of weeks before her belongings were packed and she was off to Arizona. I missed her. I lost a dance partner, a companion and a lover. She was one of the few women whose body fit seemed to complement mine so naturally. She was a playmate that I think every man should be visited with at least once in a lifetime.

Ginny and Dad, 1985

For about a year after her departure, I would curse every time I saw an Arizona license plate. But while our relationship lasted, it made up for the intimacy drought of years spent in a loveless, sexless marriage to Bernie. So once more dancing would be a sexual sublimate. In a way, dancing provides a measure of social security.

Meanwhile work at General Dynamics continued to be interesting. Nothing was ever static, not even your location. One of my building changes also involved a move into another division and product line. I was now working in the new Space Systems division.

Space Shuttle

General Dynamics was building the Space Shuttle's main cargo bay. Some very interesting technology was involved especially in the material being used for structural strength. This prompted me to add a technology component to the Management Club's educational activities. I introduced a series of technology reviews similar to the earlier technology exhibitions I conducted in Orange County. As before, it was well received. Those who felt detached from the company's engineering and manufacturing mission felt re-connected to the team.

Then a major tragedy occurred. On January 28, 1986, just 73 seconds into the launch of the Space Shuttle Challenger, the spacecraft exploded killing all aboard. Christa McAuliffe was one of the crew, the first woman teacher in space. She was selected from a field of 11,000 applicants and had planned to teach a class from space. We were watching the launch and were thunderstruck when the explosion occurred. Silence and sadness permeated the division for days. It wasn't long before the pace of operations in the Space Systems division slowed and I was transferred back to Convair and the cruise missile program. I was now part of the new Information Resource Management group involved with the analysis of new software and hardware for digitizing engineering drawings and manufacturing specifications. I attended expos and conferences around the country and had leading vendors present their technologies at our Kearney Mesa facility. The new technologies would significantly impact the way we did business – from design to manufacturing. It was an exciting time to be part of a department leading the company's venture into new technologies.

In addition to the digital conversion, we were the lead organization for introducing the latest management techniques and organizational structures. Conferences and workshops featuring management gurus such as Peter Drucker, W. Edwards Deming and Stephen Covey were springing up across the country. Company executives were sold on the value of their management principles and were more than willing to underwrite the conference fees and travel costs. As members of the Information and Management systems group, we were encouraged to attend such conferences and share what we learned upon our return. It was our job to improve company and corporate operations by training others in the management philosophies and approaches of more notable gurus.

Evidence of change resulting from the influence of Drucker, Deming and Covey was soon in evidence throughout the company. A real effort was being made to define the nature of our business, develop meaningful mission statements, focus on the quality and flatten the hierarchical pyramid. The latter had much to do with empowerment – placing the decision-making authority in the hands of those closest to the work or the problem. The new approaches provided the flexibility of much smaller organizations. It restored the responsiveness of the earlier missile activation and space race days.

Corporate management's renewed interest in re-inventing or replacing outmoded paradigms and adopting best practices even extended to authors whose works were in humanist and futurist columns. Books like Abraham Maslow's "On Management", John Naisbett's "Megatrends" and Alvin and Heidi Toffler's "Third Wave" could be found on desks throughout the company.

Robin

While attending a management conference at the Moscone Center in San Francisco, I decided to break the ice and call Robin. She was living and working in San Francisco with her husband, Steve McCamey and daughter Amber. I knew my call was out of the blue. I hadn't spoken to Robin since just before her wedding at the El Toro. Soon after their marriage, Steve was transferred from an Orange County branch Wells Fargo to San Francisco. They had been married for a few years and had bought a new home in Pacifica. When I got Robin on the phone, I invited her to dinner. She declined. It would be a several years later that we would finally get together. When we did, Robin would be divorced and sharing custody of her daughter Amber.

Perry's and Costas

During my Convair days I was a lunch regular at Perry's Restaurant in Old Town. I usually stopped there following a swim at the Point Loma YMCA. I was so consistent in my luncheon habit as well as what I would eat - rice, beans and flour tortillas - that the chefs would have my order ready from the moment I walked in. Costas had two restaurants, both named Perry's, one in San Diego's Old Town area and another, the original, in El Cajon.

Costas Georgakopoulos, a Greek-born, former accountant, owned the restaurant He had developed a very popular menu and knew how to run a business. He knew his customers, greeted them personally and led them to tables. His cooks were great and his waitresses attentive. Your coffee cup never got below the halfway mark.

Costas named the restaurant after his daughter Perry. His original restaurant in El Cajon carried the same name. Costas alternated between the two. When I lived in Pacific Beach and Del Mar, I frequented his restaurant in the Old Town area. When I lived in Santee and El Cajon, I ate at his El Cajon restaurant. Each featured the same menu. I read a lot while eating at the counter and Costas took note of my reading habits. His reading interests coincided with mine and this marked the beginning of a long exchange of ideas and reading suggestions. W. Edwards Deming and the British philosopher Charles Handy were among his favorites. A picture of Deming hung on the wall at his Old Town restaurant. I introduced him to Peter Drucker. I suspect Costas had one of the best collection of management books in the area.

Costas and I were the same age. He came to San Diego by way of Canada where he worked in the financial sector. Before he left Greece for Canada, he did his military service in the Greek army and could recall the Nazi occupation when he was a boy.

Although his background was in accounting, he wanted to run a restaurant. He purchased former restaurant properties, one in El Cajon and the other near San Diego's Old Town. He named each one "Perry's" after his daughter. As a regular customer with reading interests closely aligned with Costas', we got to know one another pretty well. We fueled each other's reading interests.

The Perry's restaurant in Old Town used to be a Denny's restaurant and a favorite stop for truckers. Its location was ideal – the juncture of Interstate 5 & Interstate 8, on the corner of Pacific and Rosecrans. He had a spacious parking lot and was just a block or two from San Diego's historic Old Town. The restaurant was open for breakfast and lunch seven days a week from 6am until 2pm. During the week, the restaurant was always full but on week-ends it was "out the doors" crowded. On Saturday and Sunday mornings people would have to line up and wait to be seated. But it was always worth the wait. The food was good, the quantity generous, the service excellent and the price reasonable.

Meantime, with Maria gone, I decided to move from Del Mar to El Cajon. Our Del Mar apartment was nice, even nicer than Pacific Beach but this move would cut my commuting time between work and dancing in half. Apart from working at General Dynamics and working out at the company gym, I was now clogging with Melinda, two stepping at the Silver Spur in El Cajon and Mulvaney's in Santee and teaching evening classes to seniors at residential retirement facilities for San Diego City College.

With all the dance socialization, it wasn't long before I was two stepping regularly with Elaine ; clogging, pistol shooting and riding horses with Lennie; and clogging and roller skating with Bonnie. All the girls were about 10-15 years my junior, all were divorced, all had kids and all had jobs. It wasn't long before my two bedroom, two bath apartment in El Cajon became a popular watering hole for my dancing friends.

Elaine

Elaine worked for a local school district, had two boys and a girl and owned her own home. She was a graduate of a California university, played the piano and guitar and had a great memory for dance steps. We danced well together and seemed to be on the same page on most issues. Later, her boys would join the Marine Corps. This made for another mini-bond. We were also close friends with one of my Convair co-workers, Dick Cree and his wife. Dick and I would attend management conferences around the country. Elaine and Dick's wife would usually see us off and greet us upon return. We also enjoyed an occasional outing on Dick's boat

Ginny Re-appears

Ginny had been living on the street and she showed it. Her clothes, hair, teeth and skin – all showed signs of neglect and too much outdoor exposure. She also wore a hooded sweat shirt as if she were hiding or shielding herself from the world. I was always glad to see her and hoped she would take advantage of available resources. Bu I couldn't get through to her. Ginny was always glad to see me. As my firstborn, she held a special place in my heart. But it broke my heart to see her reduced to this level because of her paranoia and schizophrenia.

Ginny left home a year or so before my divorce and while she was home we did our best to get help from Orange County's Mental Health department. We tried to monitor the medication the Mental Health Department prescribed but Ginny didn't like it and wouldn't take it. On one occasion we managed to get her into a county facility over a weekend, the maximum time a commitment could be made for someone in Ginny's condition. The Mental Health people were able to medicate her and calm her down. But the County could only constrain her for a limited time.. Ginny was over twenty-one and simply would not sign anything. Even as parents, we could not get power of attorney over Ginny. As the County personnel put it – "there's not much we can do unless she is a threat to herself or others. Since we don't see those factors involved, she is a free agent. That's the law."

I was totally frustrated by that law. We take better care of animals. We pick up strays, house and feed them and try to get them a home. But we let fellow humans roam the streets ill-fed, ill clothed and talking to themselves. We ignore the tragedy before our eyes. Letting persons incapable of making reasonable choices regarding their own health and mental state live aimlessly on the streets is unconscionable. What makes matters worse is the cost of care for the mentally ill. Costs are prohibitive for the average family. Unless the needed care is provided as a public service, a blind eye will continue to be turned on those helpless souls roaming the streets and talking to themselves.

It took time, even for family members, to accept the fact that Ginny really had a problem. Here was a typical eighteen year old girl, a good student, a high school graduate and working at Bob's Big Boy restaurant in Santa Ana. Then she got mixed up with a born-again religious cult in Santa Ana. She was still living home when she began talking to herself and saying she was hearing voices from somewhere. She talked about a communications net and alien forces trying to take over her body. She would let out streams of four letter words that would make a Marine blush. She developed a fetish for cleanliness. She would wipe off everything she touched or was about to touch like the phone. Then, just as suddenly as these outbursts occurred, she would revert to her sweet self. She left Bob's Big Boy and went through a series of secretarial jobs with a Temp Agency. Ginny could make a convincing appearance of normalcy when talking to people for a short period. But if you worked with her for a couple of days, elements of the schizophrenia would surface. She could only survive if her assignments were brief. She sustained herself that way for about a year then took to the streets. We lost contact. The only way I kept in touch was when she would call me and arrange a meeting usually at a restaurant like MacDonald's. Ginny always asked about her sisters, brother and mother but I was the only one she seemed to trust. Her memory was remarkably sharp but there would always be the interruption of imaginary voices

After I moved to San Diego, I kept up my meetings with Ginny. She would call me from Santa Monica and we would meet at a halfway mark between LA and San Diego like Dana Point. We would eat and spend time together, I would give her some money and clothes then we would go our separate ways. Ginny was fond of Santa Monica and that's where we met last.

I had one, out-of-the-blue encounter with Ginny while attending a conference on management systems at Marina del Rey. I had taken Elaine, a dancing friend, with me on this occasion and while driving around town one evening when who did I spot walking town the down the main street in a hooded sweatshirt? Ginny!. Talk about finding a needle in the hay stack. I hadn't seen her for months. We parked and caught up with her. She looked run down but again rejected any offer of support for housing or disability. We spent some time together over hamburgers and coffee. I brought Ginny up to date on Mark, Charlotte and Robin. We parted again with a promise to see one another again soon. Even in these painful circumstances, it was still good to see her. The next time Ginny came to San Diego, I made arrangements for her to live in a residential setting designed specifically for people with mild mental disorders. Ginny qualified for a disability allowance which would cover her rent and basic living costs. A social worker was available to help us. The place even had a piano that I thought would appeal to her. But after a tour of the place and just when it was time to sign the required paperwork, she balked. Her fear and distrust of signing anything won out. She wanted to return to Santa Monica. I was deeply disappointed. I felt inadequate. She took a bus back to Santa Monica.

Dance-Related Relationships

Meanwhile, life in San Diego went on. My relationship with Elaine was not going anywhere except for dancing although I took her kids on family outings to a camp run by General Dynamics in the local mountains near Julian. It had a swimming pool, hiking trails, horse shoe pits, cooking facilities, tents, showers and parking for trailers. Elaine and her kids enjoyed visiting the place. Elaine and I also spent a couple days without her kids in Ensenada.

Lennie, on the other hand, was something else. She was the freest spirit I ever met. The first time I met her was at our clogging club in El Cajon. I was intrigued by someone who didn't seem to fit the mold – at least dress-wise. She wore a biker get-up including frayed jeans and a black leather jacket. She also drove a motorcycle. But she was as sweet as they come. She was from Spring Valley and had a ranch mentality. In fact, she lived across the street from a horse ranch where she boarded and trained horses. Her specialty was restoring horses to service that had been abused or spooked. She was a "horse whisperer" of sorts. She also cared for some horses used by Sheriff volunteers on back country patrols. She got me up on a horse one night for a ride through the Otay Mesa hills. Her Australian sheep dog guided us along the dark paths and through breaks in a fence. It was a memorable experience. It happened to on July 4th and from our vantage point we could watch firework displays from Imperial Beach and Coronado to San Diego bay and Mission Beach.

Lennie also enjoyed pistol shooting and we would use a small arms range used by the Sheriff and sometimes a private range for practice. We would fire away with a 38 and 45 that she owned. It was a long time since I was on a pistol range and my shooting proved it. Lennie was a better shot. She also fished and would catch fish in places I couldn't believe fish would inhabit. She was a real "live off the land" girl. She also had a lovely daughter about ten years old. Last I heard Lennie was working on a County road construction crew. Sounds like Lennie. She could hold her own with most men on anything.

Bonnie was a solidly built blond, about 5'5, an enthusiastic clogger and an energetic skater. She was a registered nurse or physical therapist, maybe both. Bonnie as well as Elaine and Lennie were all physically active girls who enjoyed the outdoors. But Bonnie was the only skater. I enjoyed skating on the concrete sidewalks along Mission and Pacific Beach. We both used regular four wheel skates or quads rather than in-line skates. One of my favorite exercise routines was running on the sand from Mission Beach to Pacific Beach with a skate in each hand then skating back on the return trip. Although Bonnie didn't join me on the beach runs, we did get together on occasion for a Sunday morning skate at Pacific Beach.

But time was running out for me and others as the 1987 Intermediate Range Nuclear Forces Treaty resulted in the destruction of ground launch cruise missiles and their launch mechanisms. Later, General Dynamics would sell its remaining contract for the Tomahawk cruise missile, launched from ships and submarines, to Raytheon and McDonnell Douglas.

Chapter 7

The NINETIES

Some of the highlight events of the nineties included the Gulf War, German reunification, launch of the Hubble space telescope, the Panama invasion, release of Nelson Mandela from a South African prison, the demise of Yugoslavia, the dismantling of the Soviet Union, racial riots in LA over Rodney King's beating, the Waco Tragedy, NAFTA ratification, World Trade Center explosion, Black Hawk down in Somalia, North Korean nuclear violations, Ruanda genocide, Tiger Woods wins Masters, Oklahoma City bombing, affirmative action scuttled, Rabin assassinated, Unabomber arrested, OJ trial, Lance Armstrong diagnosed with cancer, Dolly cloned, Mother Theresa dies, India and Pakistan resume nuclear tests, Columbine school shooting, Panama Canal returned, Euro created and a military coup in Pakistan.

Downsizing

The handwriting that was on the wall in the eighties materialized in the nineties with the shut down of General Dynamics main missile and aerospace engineering and manufacturing facilities at Kearney Mesa. It was a sad day for thousands. So many had worked for General Dynamics for such a long time that it had become a major part of their lives. Now it was gone. I had planned to work at least another 10-15 years because there was no mandatory retirement age. I had envisioned a retirement income sufficient to facilitate other pursuits like writing, teaching, school formation and traveling. But immediately following the downsizing, I knew I would have to supplement my income almost immediately. One way to decrease my monthly expenses was to cut my monthly living expenses. This would mean sharing living quarters with someone. That first someone was Marsha.

Marsha

Marsha, like most of my other women dance associates, was about 10-15 years my junior and liked to dance. She also owned her own condo, had a grown adopted son and a married, adopted daughter. After a few months of dancing and going to the movies together, we decided that a joint living venture made good sense economically. I moved in.

Meantime, although I was sending an occasional resume to Political Science departments or local governments, I was also trying to sell my Educational Service Corps concept. This Corps would be a model expeditionary force of educators committed to assisting public schools adopt more effective teaching practices. It would be accomplished through a series of demonstrations at select schools. The demonstrations would reflect the techniques being used in the more successful schools at home and abroad. This would require extensive global travel to study teaching practices abroad and demonstrate them at home. This was a modification of my earlier proposal for a US Academy of Education. Unfortunately, I could never attract sufficient attention from the US Department of Education to sponsor the concept.

Somerton

Of the many resumes I was sending out those days, one ended up on the mayor's desk in Somerton, Arizona. The mayor was a middle aged woman with a slight Spanish inflection who also served on the school board. She had been looking for a new manager for several months. Some internal squabbles led to a parting of the ways with the last manager. The mayor was looking for someone with no prior connection to their internal affairs but with prior city government experience. After a couple phone calls, an interview with the mayor was scheduled. The challenge of being the city's top administrator, however small the city, appealed to me. The manager position was the pinnacle and prized destination of most who took a master's in Public Administration although civil engineering, law enforcement, planning and finance were also among the more typical backgrounds for the job.

When I interviewed for the job, the mayor told me there was a house I could use near one of the many lettuce fields surrounding the city. Lettuce was a major crop in Somerton. But that offer was quickly withdrawn. It seems one of the council members noted that the house was outside the city limits. The council wanted the manager to live within the city limits. So housing was a problem for me from the beginning. After a couple weeks living in a local motel, I took up residence in a trailer park just a couple blocks from the city hall. I lived there during the week and returned home to Santee on week-ends.

It was obvious from the beginning that there was internal friction among the council members and a cozy relationship between the Mayor and the City Clerk. I remember one city employee approaching me with a friendly warning. "You're lucky if you last a month." That remark sounded a warning bell. I never did get a satisfactory answer about the reasons for the previous manager's departure, not even from the manager himself when I finally met him.

Yuma's city attorney was on contract to Somerton as its city attorney. He gave me a friendly warning about the city clerk who wanted the manager job for herself and about the in-fighting on the city council. That in-fighting led to my hiring. It seems the mayor and council wanted someone detached from the city's past; someone who would just run the city in a professional manner. For several months before my arrival, the city was without a full time leader. The major and city council provided minimal oversight to the various departments but, for the most part, heads operated independently.

I knew the job had its pitfalls but the opportunity the job presented as a stepping stone to future city manager jobs back in San Diego or Orange County outweighed the risky settings. Holding the actual position of city manager had a certain value. It's one thing to be a staffer; it's quite another to actually hold the manager position.. It meant reporting directly to the mayor and city council, helping shape policy and executing it. A lot of power resides in the hands of mayors, councilmembers and city managers. Planning, zoning, utility rates, contract services, hiring, salaries, employee benefits and, if a charter city, even taxes are within their power. Just a week or so after I was hired, Somerton was holding its annual parade. I was asked to ride in the parade and I did so with Marsha. Unfortunately my exit was not quite as triumphant as my entrance.

One of my first major tasks for the city was to put together a budget for the next fiscal year. This would give me the opportunity to highlight the priorities that lay ahead. Such things as expanding the city's water storage capacity, modernizing an outmoded sewage treatment facility, replacing worn-out vehicles and improving street maintenance were high on my list. Other recommendations included the possibility of acquiring health insurance for a city of 10,000, a new city hall and a vigorous campaign to attract businesses. Yuma was the biggest city nearby and the Marines also had an air station there. Somerton's economic mainstays included agriculture (mostly lettuce), government and public utility jobs, golfing ranges, trailer parks and "snow birds". The "snow birds" were retirees for the most part who came to Arizona to escape the cold of northern states and Canada during the fall, winter and spring. I was anxious to attract new business. I remember a little kid coming up to me after a community meeting.

"Hey, Mr. Manager, when are we going to get McDonald's here?

All I could answer was "We're working on it, son". Being able to attract popular fast restaurants to a community as small as Somerton would be a challenge. Fast food marketers would know when to make their move. It would be a matter of traffic counts, revenue projections, and city development plans.

Somerton, although small town USA, was a full service city. It provided its own police, fire, public works and recreation. It had a golf course, a crop duster airfield and an Indian gaming casino on its border. Lettuce was its primary crop. Flown out of Yuma on one day, it could be for sale on European vegetable stalls the next. But like many small towns, a lot of problems found their way to the manager's office. My first brush with a small town problem involved the school, the city and the state.

A student was passed over for an award for the DARE (drug abuse resistance education) program and the parents complained. The police insisted that the student did not meet the requirements. The parents disagreed. After several meetings between the parties involved without resolution, the issue was passed on to the State level DARE program. There, a ruling came down in the police department's favor. But this was not a win-win situation. In a small town, frictions become public knowledge quickly. Others problems presented to the city council were usually resolved on a council vote unless it was a close split. That almost guaranteed the animosity would continue. Such is the nature of life in a democracy, especially at the local level. At least the council meetings in Somerton were held in English even though the racial composition was 90% Mexican. A few miles down the road, the US town of San Luis which bordered Mexico held its council meetings in Spanish.

Sometimes a manager is directed by a mayor or council to take action that most managers would normally do on their own. One such directed action that involved the police chief's wearing of his uniform probably accelerated his departure. In some cities, police chiefs have the option to wear civilian clothes or a uniform. That option had been in place in Somerton until the mayor felt the chief should wear his uniform. I told the chief of the mayor's desire and let it go at that. I felt that action to insist on this was petty. In my previous local government experience, police chiefs had the option of wearing or not wearing their uniform as they chose. The same mayor also insisted in taking a new police car to attend a conference in Phoenix when regular city vehicles were available. This caused quite a stir among the police department. I advised the mayor that using a new police vehicle to attend a conference in Phoenix was ill advised and against my wishes as well as the police department. Despite objections, the mayor took the new police vehicle.

I also had my own misgivings about certain police activities. One involved the assignment of one of our officers to a joint agency task forces for drug interdiction. Officers on such teams worked undercover, crossed jurisdictional lines and were seldom seen in their home departments. It was hard to reconcile the significance of a full time commitment from a city as small as our own. On one of the few occasions I saw this officer, he recommended I see a movie that would give me some real insight into the drug world. The movie was called "American Me" starring James Olmos. It was playing in Yuma's only theatre and I went to see it. It gave me a better understanding of the world that these officers worked in but I still felt our police force was too small to be contributing a full time officer.

In the interest of keeping operating costs down, I explored the possibility of subcontracting our police function to the Yuma County Sheriff. I also considered subcontracting fire and emergency medical service to Rural Metro a private company. This company was already serving Yuma. As you might imagine, reviewing the cost advantage of contracting to a private competitive source was not popular with the staff of affected departments even though this was a common practice among many small cities. But Somerton liked being a full service city and preferred having these basic functions under their direct control. In other areas, like trash collection, street repair and vehicle maintenance there was no objection.

About this time, a new book, "Reinventing Government" was making its way into city halls across the country. One of its authors, Ted Gaebler, was on the speaking circuit promoting the book and selling its major ideas. Those ideas promoted the introduction of more competition between private and public entities in providing tax-funded services. I met Ted Gaebler at a Managers Conference in Phoenix where he was the keynote speaker. It was exciting to meet the man whose book was causing such a stir in city halls across the country. The book challenged paradigms that thwarted innovation; paradigms that kept most governmental services off-limits to the private sector. It called for making competition between public and private services a key element in determining the best shake for the tax dollar. The book and Ted Gaebler's speaking engagements were stirring up "reinvention" fever across the country. The management dicta of gurus like Drucker and Deming were also becoming popular in the public sector. I conducted several related seminars for my department heads, a new experience for many in this small, agriculturally-oriented community.

Shortly after I met Ted Gaebler, I had the opportunity to meet Senator John McCain. McCain was spending a couple days in Yuma reviewing local conditions. I spent two days at these meetings that were well attended. At the first day's meeting at a question and answer forum, I introduced myself, asked a question and got his answer. The next day when I rose to ask another question, McCain said "Hi, Bob" before I could give my name. I couldn't believe he remembered my name among all the people he met those two days. When I shared this experience with a fellow participant, he told me that McCain developed his remarkable memory while captive in Vietnam.

Back at city hall, my relations with the mayor and city clerk were blowing hot and cold. I was getting fed up with being undercut by a city clerk and mayor whose actions were undercutting my job and destroying trust. Nor did I appreciate things being added to the council's agenda without first informing me. I was also getting fed up with my living accommodations. I took to reading the biographies of military leaders like Patton and MacArthur to steel myself for continuing or resigning. I read several Patton biographies including those by Carlo D'Este, Martin Blumenson and Ladislas Farago. I also re-read MacArthur's autobiography "Reminiscences". I felt my job and, by extension, the job of other managers was being compromised. I still had the support of a majority of council members but a split was apparent. I was on the brink of throwing in the towel and would have had not one of my council friends persuaded me to stay. The whole relationship environment reminded me of the story about the city manager who was hospitalized with a heart problems being visited by a council member "Hi, John" the council member said. "Hope you are feeling well. The council voted a special get-well resolution last night." As the council member turned to leave the room, he said "By the way, the vote was 4-3".

A majority of my council members understood my discontent and that I was thinking of resigning. My friends on the council urged me to stay. I was not on contract so separation would be simple. I sensed little prospect for a long term relationship. I would prepare a budget for the coming year and that would be it.

Meanwhile I found my own stress-relieving outlets by jogging, swimming at Yuma's municipal plunge, dancing occasionally at a country western bar and eating in Yuma's restaurants. Yuma was just 10 minutes down the road from Somerton.. At the time, the San Diego Padres were using Yuma for their spring training and I enjoyed watching some of their practice sessions. One of Yuma's more notable tourist attractions was its Territorial Prison. This landmark was occasionally used for on location shots in the filming of western movies. The desert landscape surrounding the prison was so forbidding that escape attempts were minimal.

It wasn't long before my dancing interests resulted in a link-up with a small group of two-steppers who frequented a Yuma bar with a dance floor.. Lillian was one of the dancers who worked at the State Employment Development department in Yuma. She was about the only person I could talk to with any sense of confidentiality about my work in Somerton. Lillian had a good grasp of the local economy and the income maintenance process that kept so many farm laborers on a payroll. Workers would switch from farm payrolls to unemployment benefits with minimal lapses in between.

On week-ends I would be back to San Diego with Marsha. The week-ends were usually rest and recreation times for us. I would come home with flowers in hand. We would go dancing, perhaps take in a movie and eat out. San Diego was a real oasis compared to Yuma and Somerton.. With its zoo, Sea World, Balboa Park, beaches, sea sports, nearby mountains and mild climate, San Diego is a Mecca for industry, tourism and retirement. How many times can you visit the Yuma Territorial prison?

On the other hand, Phoenix is a delightful cosmopolitan area. It is also a center for many week-end dancing events ranging from country western to west coast swing. Tucson is another beautiful spot in the middle of a desert dominated by suguaro cactus.and golf courses. It was also the home, museum and shop of Arizona's famous artist,Ted De Grazia, Of Italian ancestry and born in Arizona before it became a state, DeGrazia is known for many works. His painting of Los Ninos, a circle of dancing children of the Southwest is among his best known works. The popularity of this painting spread when it was used on UNICEF Christmas cards. Bernie loved that painting and displayed it prominently in both our Redlands and Anaheim homes.

On Marsha's last visit to Phoenix I had to break the news of my severance sooner than I had expected. Although she was aware of the issues underlying my discomfort and my relationship with the mayor and clerk, the news that I was no longer working for Somerton put a damper on our week-end. But life goes on. We took in a movie, went dancing, spent the night in Phoenix and returned to San Diego the next day. I would soon be involved once again in educational activities.

London, Paris, Brussels and Amsterdam

Marsha liked to travel. So did I. But like many San Diego residents we were well aware of San Diego's amenities like climate, scenery and things to do. The zoo, beaches, Balboa Park, Sea World, museums, local mountains, hiking, biking, swimming, fishing, schools, theatre and music – we had it all.. This minimized our travel needs. But a change of pace and scenery can rejuvenate one's outlook and expand one's perspective regardless of a favored permanent residence. Besides, Europe did have treasures of the Old World that the New could ever match like the British museums, the Eiffel Tower, Versailles and the Champs Elysees.

Marsha and I had different objectives in mind while traveling. Although we both shared the enjoyment of new sights and sounds, Marsha had a special interest in beads and I had a special interest in making a video documentary of our trip. She had a significant bead collection and never tired of searching out new sources. She had the same built-in radar for bead shops that I had for dancing spots. She could find small bead shops in London and Brussels that even those born there would never find. As for me, armed with my new Panasonic camcorder, I got my fill of videotaping all the historic sights and sounds. From the Tower of London, Westminster Abbey and the British museum to the Champs Elysees, the Eiffel Tower, Versailles, Notre Dame, the Louvre, the linens of Brussels and the cheese making and windmills of Holland. We were part of a tour group and really got around. After the tour, we decided to spend a few more days on our own in Paris before crossing the Channel and flying back on Virgin Atlantic. I had hours of videotape that I could share with students of history and World Affairs. Marsha got home with the beads and bobbins she wanted for her sewing.

Palomar College

It wasn't long before I was linked to Palomar Community College. The college was looking for an outreach teacher who could bring courses like Current Events and World Affairs to seniors living in residential retirement residences. I applied and within a few weeks of returning from Somerton and enjoying an overseas holiday, I was in a teaching mode once again. I expanded the reach of these programs to several retirement residences in the Escondido-Poway-Rancho Bernardo areas.

These education programs were the best deal in town and a win-win situation for all. Like most public education programs, State reimbursement was based on student head counts. So there were always minimal attendance requirements to ensure coverage of the teacher salary. These off-site courses were very cost effective and beneficial to the resident. The governing school district was spared the expense of maintenance and utilities and the participants enjoyed the by-products of the mental stimulation and interaction. Participants enjoyed sharing their opinions and interacting with others and re-connecting to a sense of citizenship. The program had particular appeal to those who were college educated and former professionals. It also appealed to those who were readers, enjoyed keeping up with the news and enjoyed the social interaction of a seminar style environment.

Building a class of students who could contribute to the discussions and tolerate opposing opinions was not always easy. It was my experience that only about 10 per cent of a retirement community population would be interested. If minimal attendance requirements were to be met, a residence would need a population of about two hundred to meet a goal of 15-20 students. Some facilities were so anxious to host these programs they would assist non-ambulatory residents get to class to ensure attendance requirements were met. One thing I learned to appreciate, however, was that despite physical limitations and advanced years many were remarkably sharp in assessing things taking place domestically and internationally.

In addition to the outreach programs of the community colleges, there were other foundations supporting the goal of lifelong learning for seniors. Osher and Oasis both provide intellectually stimulating classes for individuals over fifty. Costs are minimal and classes are conducted at convenient times and locations. Osher classes are usually conducted on a university campus such as San Diego State, Cal State San Marcos and the University of California-San Diego. Oasis classes are sponsored and take place in a Macy department store. Instructors are compensated at approximately the same rate as a community college adjunct. I've conducted programs for both organizations and I have also worked independently. I've worked independently for years at the Redwood Town Center in Escondido. When budget cutbacks forced the curtailment of the outreach programs, the Redwood Town Center residents insisted the program continue. I was requested to continue the course as a private contractor. The course continues to this day.

In-Cahoots

I owe my introduction to In-Cahoots to two close friends of Marsha's, Cindy and Bob. These two enjoyed country dancing as much as we. While attending one of their dinner parties at their new condo in Mission Valley, they suggested we go dancing at a new western bar not far from where they lived. We did and that was our introduction to the most popular country site in San Diego – In-Cahoots.

In Cahoots is located in Mission Valley and has been the area's top spot for two-step and line dancing since the early nineties. Free dance lessons, a tight sized dance floor, continuous music and reasonably priced food and drinks make it one of most popular wat4ering holes around. It is open every night except Mondays Two dances are taught each night, one a line dance, the other a couple. Lessons begin at 6:30pm sharp with each lesson taking about thirty minutes.

For all its fun and exercise, the In Cahoots' experience is the most reasonable entertainment deal in town. Its rib-eye steak, baked potato and glass of beer is one of the best deals in town.. If you don't drink, there are plenty of non-alcoholic beverages. And, if you participate in most of the line and couple dances, you'll get a workout that could match any gym's.

Although the line dancers outnumber the couple dancers, there are usually enough of each to keep the dance floor comfortably occupied although sometimes overcrowded. You might also find a smattering of other dances sprinkled throughout the night like the waltz, nite-club two-step, cowboy cha cha, jitterbug swing and, when the music is right, some West Coast swing in the dance floor corners.

Teaching West Coast swing, however, is taboo at In-Cahoots.. The management considers West Coast inconsistent with the western motif. But West Coast has long eclipsed East Coast swing in popularity. It is featured at most country dance competitions and country workshops. But West Coast is danced to more contemporary music with a beat closer to that of Michael Jackson's Thriller. Major country workshops take place several times a year, usually at a large hotel with dance floors large enough to accommodate a couple hundred dancers. JD Dougherty, one of San Diego's best known country instructors, produces many dance workshops and competitions. Ronnie DeBenedetta, a national two-step champion who works out of Michael Kiehm's Starlight Ballroom, is a dominant figure on the country dance scene, both nationally and internationally.

If you don't have a partner or don't care for couple dancing, line dancing is as ideal as clogging and folk dancing. With line dancing, although you learn as a group and dance as a group, you are really a solo performer. Unlike couple dancing, there is seldom any physical connection with other dancers - no belt holds, no hand holds, no shoulder holds, no body contact and only occasional eye contact. While this may reflect a culture of independent ruggedness, everyone executes the same steps although there is plenty of room for self-expression. Spins, high leg kicks and hip gyrations make some dancers stand out. Unlike square dancing and clogging, line dancing does not use a caller but it does require memorizing the steps. When done frequently enough, the steps get burned into a dancer's memory. Moves like triple step, step drag, Monterey turn, sailor shuffle, kick ball change, jazz square, syncopated grape vine, quarter turn, etc. become second nature. Most line dances reflect a combination of such moves. The more proficient dancers are those who dance frequently. I enjoy learning new dances because I believe this keeps me alert and receptive to change. I also think that learning new dances and reviewing old ones help condition you for extended time on the dance floor.

The dress at In-Cahoots is casual. For girls, levis, shorts, western style skirts, and boots are popular. For guys, it's levis, a western shirt, boots and sometimes a hat. Overall, the rule is to dress comfortably for a night of movement. The ambiance at In-Cahoots also makes it ideal for celebrating birthdays and other special occasions A table ringed with balloons and a large cake as a centerpiece is a frequent sight.

Like most western bars, the dance floor and drinking are the core activites.. Tables and chairs ring the floor. In-Cahoots has a main bar and two satellite bars. The main bar is on the ground floor. A second bar is on a split level that rings the dance floor. The third bar is on a second floor where the seating also overlooks the dance floor. Several pool tables are also on this level. There is also an outdoor patio where burgers and typical side dishes are served during summer months. Getting a table on the ground floor near the entrances to the dance floor is the choicest location. This requires getting to In-Cahoots early to stake your claim on the more desirable tables. Tables and chairs fill up quickly.

When it comes to personalities, In-Cahoots has its share. The Who's Who of In-Cahoots would make a long list. But some of the regulars I've known over the years would include the following:

Jimmy, an octogenarian and WWII bomber pilot was a regular for years until recently. He knew all the dances, had a great western wardrobe that changed every night and gave In-Cahoots its share of drinking patronage. On Friday or Saturday nights, Jimmy would usually show up in a coat and tie, his standard attire for Temple services. If you ask Jimmy about his preference for a dance partner, he will tell you he prefers older women who have been dancing for awhile. He finds many of the younger women lacking in dancing skills he appreciates. Although Jimmy has not been seen at the club of late, he is remembered by the many who knew him

Joanne has been a patron since the club first opened.in the early nineties. Until her husband passed away, they were country dance regulars. They were among the first patrons of In-Cahoots- Mission Valley. Although

Joanne's husband has passed on, Joanne and her daughter Linda carry on the family dancing tradition. Joanne is usually the anchor for our favorite table which is the ground level close to the dance floor entry. We usually get the same table thanks to Mikey, another long-time patron and friend of Joanne's. We are so accustomed to using the same table that if someone else beats us to it, it throws us off-balance.

Linda, Joanne's daughter, is an enthusiastic dancer, lively instructor, and member of the dance team. When she couple dances, she likes to spin. It's hard to believe that Linda is retired Air Force. She looks like an early twenty something or teenager. It is also hard to believe that she is shorter than her mother Joanne.

Mikey is another regular who generally gets to In-Cahoots just as it opens in early evening and secures our favorite table. Mikey enjoys an occasional couple dance such as the Cowboy cha Cha, the Jitterbug swing and even a West Coast swing. Mikey has been a fixture for years and if he or Joanne are a no-shows, others will occupy our favorite table.

For all the years we dancers have known one another, we still stumble over names. I am one of the worst. At some dance centers, dancers wear name tags. Not so at In-Cahoots. Although I know most of the regulars by sight, a continuing rush to the dance floor relegates name recall to secondary importance. I find it much easier to remember the name of a couple dance partner than that of individuals who only line dance. With line dancers, physical contact is minimal or non-existent and you seldom face one another. You are a face in a crowd. When you couple dance, there is time for a little chit-chat and name exchange. If your couple dance is enjoyable and you would like to repeat the performance, an effort is usually made to remember your partner's name.

Other dancers I have associated with over the years include:

Soon is a very pretty South Korean who lives in Coronado, drives a red Mercedes convertible and has been a regular at In-Cahoots for as long as I can remember. She not only knows most the line dances but is an excellent couple dancer as well. Her beauty and grace are ageless. I enjoy dancing with her.

Stephanie is an employee of the Sycuan Indian Reservation who has been dancing at In-Cahoots for as long as I can remember.. She has a steel trap mind when it comes to remembering the line dances. She prefers line dancing to couple dancing and is one of the sweetest persons you could ever meet.

Frank is a retired San Diego Port District employee who dances almost nightly. He was born in Ireland as the Irish lilt in his speech will affirm. He enjoys couple dancing in all its forms including country, ballroom, and west coast swing. He generally eschews line dancing using the line to discuss current events while sizing up the girls dancing for his next couple dance partner selection. He will graciously give you his opinion on a wide variety of topics. But Frank comes to dance and is popular with many of the better girl dancers.

Bob, a former chiropractor turned gardener, is one of the more vigorous couple dancers at In-Cahoots. He eschews line dancing but makes up for it with his energetic couple dancing. Any girl who dances with Bob is guaranteed a work-out. Bob likes to integrate swing movements with the two-step. His choice of dance partner is usually someone who can keep up with his energetic moves.

Mark is a Postal employee who brings high energy dancing to In-Cahoots after a full day of mail delivery. You might think dancing would be one of the last things on his mind after his work day but not Mark. Like others who spend a lot of time on their feet, they develop an unbelievable endurance. Mark prefers couple dancing to line dancing and seldom misses an evening or a couple dance. He is popular with the girls and is sought-after for a two -step and west coast swing. His engaging personality wins him many friends and dance partners.

Steve is an accountant, who takes his dancing seriously and dances with a style that is uniquely his including hat flipping tricks. He also dances with a partner who accommodates his moves very well. Steve has invested a lot time creating the routines that make him a standout.

Charlotte and Robin, 1991

Charlotte and daughter Aryn 1998

Jim is a practicing attorney who enjoys both line and couple dancing punctuated with a beer or two. His pretty wife, also a good dancer, gave him a daughter not too long ago. Apart from his legal affairs and dancing, Jim serves as a fire-fighting volunteer with a winged and helicopter aircraft group that makes water drops on fires that plague Southern California especially in the San Diego county area.

Don and his wife Kay have been on country dance scene as long as I can remember. Don is a former naval pilot who had significant responsibilities during the Cuban Missile Crisis of 1962. He has written a book about his Cuban episode experience. A retired naval officer and successful business owner, Don continues to pursue many unique interests but always finds time to dance. Both he and his wife Kay enjoy both line and couple dancing.

Charlie is our good humor man with a contagious smile and a boisterous laugh. Except when dancing, he can usually be found roaming the dance hall with a beer in hand. He is an enthusiastic couple dancer and takes to line dancing as well.

Stewart is tall, heavy set, and generous to a fault. He is a contributor of many of the goodies brought into In-Cahoots whether for a birthday or just to make it an occasion. He does quite well on the dance floor and prefers line dancing.

Mitch is retired, reserved and has been on the dance circuit for some time. He prefers the couple dances and enjoys splitting his time between conversations with friends and two stepping.

Mike is the tall, lanky, horse-loving cowboy who manages the bar and keeps things humming. He keeps a winning formula of dancing, drinking and eating in play to the non-stop sounds of country music. As if that were not enough, a series of TV monitors ring the bar and are tuned to the latest sporting events.

The Dance Team

In-Cahoots has a dance team that rehearses and performs at community events throughout the year and helps conduct the nightly dance teaching. Until recently, Ellen was the director, choreographer and lead instructor. The team is outfitted in attractive western gear and features about twenty dancers, men and women. Whenever the team performs for In-Cahoot's patrons, they leave the floor to the sound of cheers and rousing applause.

Some of Ellen's main dance instructors include Linda, Shawndolynn, Jen, Stephanie,and Sue.

The Others

It seems almost every bar has a few individuals whose distinctive personalities set them apart. Sandy, also no longer a bar presence, liked to commandeer a table and surround himself with good-looking women. In his late sixties, he made no bones about his preference for young, attractive women. He was a master at staking out a table and reserving it for all the young women he could corral. His trade mark outfit was levis, sneakers and a baseball cap. Standing about 6'2", he had one of the few voices that can be heard over the music. He occasionally took to the dance floor to show a novice dancer how to two-step. He was opinionated, self-assured, and would give you his opinion on any topic at the drop of a hat.

Tom was noted for his scent of cologne and a perpetual smile. With marriage prospects often in play on the dance circuit, Tom took the plunge. Best I can tell, his marriage still holds but I haven't seen him at In-Cahoots for some time.

Population Diversity

In-Cahoots patrons span the range of professions and ages. Its clientele includes lawyers, teachers, military, professionals, executives and retirees - an unique cross-section of the San Diego community.

Dance Instruction

Thanks to Ellen, teaching line dancing has become a standardized process at In-Cahoots. About six different girls, all members of the dance team, serve as instructors and all use the same method. That method entails teaching segments of a dance incrementally with frequent reviews of earlier segments until the entire dance is learned. The continuous repetition reinforces memory and motor skills.

Class sizes usually range from 40 to 60 students broken into four or six row of about ten each. The instructor alternates rows frequently so that everyone get an opportunity to view the instructor's footwork. Within a matter of 20 to 30 minutes, a dance can be thoroughly taught. When the instructor is satisfied the group can execute the complete dance satisfactorily, the music is played. The dancers get the opportunity to practice the dance to three songs. Later in the evening, just before a couple dance lesson begins, the dancers get the opportunity to review the same line dance again. This technique has proven very effective at In-Cahoots.

Most of the line dances have catchy titles taken from popular tunes: Dizzy, Alley Cat, Good Times, Hustle Bustle, Take Me Down, City Slicker, Four on the Floor, Beer on the Table, Dancin' Feet, Chill Factor, Watermelon Crawl, Crazy Legs, Walkin' Wazi, Whiskey Drinkin' and Walk the Line. Specific line dances are usually matched to specific songs but not always. The disk jockey will usually announce the name of the line dance and provide a countdown for starting the dance. A dedicated line dancer might know more than fifty line dances. If an individual does both couple and line dances, he or she could be on the dance floor all night. The more dances you do, the more exercise you get. An hour or two of steady dancing is the equal to any vigorous aerobic routine.

Our Santee residence was ideally situated for countywide country dancing. Mulvaney's was on one end of town; the Renegade on the other. Mulvaney's which recently closed, was also known as the Wagon Wheel. It had one of the best dance floors in the area. The Renegade, on the other hand, was much smaller than Mulvaney's, has the ambiance of a local bar and a small rectangular dance floor. But In-Cahoots remains the hands-down favorite. Its vibrancy, crowd, right-sized dance floor and mid-town location make it the number one country dance spot in San Diego.

Management Symposia

With budget cutbacks affecting the number of course offerings at Community Colleges, my educational interests shifted to management conferences, prototype programs for middle schools, and a demonstration of a proposed new charter school. It was time to re-apply my experience in industry, government and schools. Perry's and Jimmy's restaurants in El Cajon and Santee would now be the staging area for developing our plans and recruiting likeminded individuals.

My new friends, most of whom were seniors, had the drive of individuals half their age. What eventually emerged from our watering hole at Perry's was a think tank. It provided a center for refining ideas and putting them in motion.

Our planning group reflected a broad range of expertise - US history, socio-economics, international affairs, management, education, and engineering. We were a 20th-21st century version of Benjamin Franklin's book and discussion club during the pre-revolutionary days in Philadelphia. And, just as my Somerton days turned me towards a study of Patton and MacArthur to steel my own actions, our discussions invigorated our interests in things that had to be done in much the same was as our founders during pre-revolutionary times. I learned more about the origins of our founding by reading good biographies of Washington, Franklin, Adams, Jefferson, Madison and Hamilton than I ever learned from textbooks. In fact, I came to view the typical history textbook with its jumble of photos, chopped up layouts, questions, projects, bulky size and heavy weight as an impediment to learning.

As my World Affairs program expanded, so did my reading regimen. My interest in management and educational affairs was coupled with my interests in political and foreign affairs. I was in the habit of reading Time, Newsweek, US New & World Report, the Economist, Fortune, Forbes and the Wall Street Journal. I was hooked on CSPAN and the military channel. Peter Drucker, W. Edwards Deming, Abraham Maslow, Jack Welch, Lee Iacoco and Stephen Covey were among my favorite management authors. I was also an adherent to the philosophy and perspective of Viktor Frankl, Charles Handy and Mortimer Adler. If I overlooked any significant publication, my Greek restauranteur friend Costas was there as my backstop. I trusted his reading recommendations and he trusted mine. The combination of business, education and management experience gave our planning group a unique edge. We had morphed into a mini think tank.

Costas nurtured our interests more than he realized. His constant introduction of new material prodded us to keep abreast of recent releases. Although Costas often expressed his frustration in not being able to express himself as well in English as he could in Greek, he always managed to get his points across. Sometimes I wished I were fluent in Greek. But Costas' had a steel-trap mind. I don't know how many times he would draw my attention to a particular passage in a book we were both reading even giving me the page it was on. I think he had a photographic memory.

It wasn't long before our coffee-laced discussions resulted in action plans. Just as the Revolutionary patriots of old found the New England taverns convenient for stoking the fires of change, our planning group used Perry's in much the same way. Frank Nakamura, Harry Vorrath and myself were the nucleus of this action group. Bob Mendoza would join us later.

Frank Nakamura

Frank was a business manager, mechanical engineer and industrial supply representative who stood slightly over five feet. He spent his high school years in a Japanese internment camp at Poston, Arizona. There would be ten such camps in operation during WWII. Poston was the largest housing about 17,000 Japanese Americans forced to live there during the war. Del Webb, a name well known in San Diego for his housing developments including Sun City in Riverside County, was the camp's architect and builder. Ironically, Poston was built on Indian land over their objections. Frank and his family, Imperial Valley farmers, were rounded up and shipped there during the early days of WWII on the basis of FDR's executive order. However, during WWII, a Japanese combat regiment was allowed to form and fight in Europe. It was the most highly decorated unit in the US Army.

At the end of WWII, Frank, an outstanding student both in Imperial County and Poston, decided to attend the University of Michigan. At Michigan, Frank became the first Japanese American to make the first string, varsity football team. He majored in mechanical engineering with a minor in education.

I met Frank at the La Mesa YMCA where both of us swam daily. At the time, Frank was a manufacturer's representative for machine oils but prior to that he was the manufacturing manager for Buck Knives in El Cajon. He also held a comparable position at a plant in the Los Angeles area. Our locker room conversations and mutual interests led to a lasting friendship. It wasn't long before Frank was a regular at our breakfast or lunch meetings at Perry's. His knowledge and even temperament made Frank a prized member of our group. His common sense input was valued. I found it remarkable that Frank never showed a trace of bitterness about Poston although he endured many deprivations there. He was one of the most positive and upbeat persons I ever knew.

Harry Vorrath

Harry and I had a couple things in common. We both served in the US Marine Corps about the same time and both had a strong religious influence in our background. Harry was born in Canada where he attended high school then came to the US where he joined the Marine Corps. After separation from the Corps, Harry attended theological seminaries in Iowa and Ohio. He was a natural leader and a very capable Dutchman. He even spoke Dutch and got a chance to use it during Oktoberfest celebrations at a German-American club in his neighborhood.

I don't recall the circumstances of our first meeting but it was probably at Perry's in El Cajon. I made several friends there either through breakfast-counter conversations or introduction by Costas. But among my many acquaintances, Harry was one I would put in my cherished friend column. He was the founder of a behavioral modification program for troubled youth and the author of a book on the subject called "Positive Peer Culture". We shared mutual educational interests although our approaches varied. He was results- oriented, results that could be measured by observable behavior change in problem students. His program changed the behavior in hard-to-manage youth from negative to positive. He had an impressive track record in institutions across the country. The essence of his program was getting his students to consider the needs of others rather than selfishly considering only their own wants. At the time of our meeting, Harry was partially retired. But like so many mission-driven individuals, traditional retirement was out of the question for Harry. He was still consulting with several institutions in the mid-west.

Frank, Harry and I were a regular trio at Perry's. Other regulars got to know us and some joined our discussion group. We welcomed others to our circle and enjoyed the stimulus of fresh ideas. To be sure, we had our differences but never to the point of diverting ourselves from developing a positive plan of action. Harry's plate was usually full given the success of his program and the success of his book. The book was now in print in several countries abroad as well as at home. He resumed consulting for several Midwest institutions. Whenever Harry was out-of-town, others slotted themselves into our discussion group. Given the scope of our topics, we never wanted for participants.

But East County also had a reputation for Red Necks, especially Lakeside. There were also some racial incidents in Santee. Both Santee and Lakeside were considered among the "whitest" areas in the county. Roy, a regular customer at Perry's came as close to a Red Neck profile as anyone. He lived in Lakeside, worked for a San Diego shipbuilder and was a licensed pyro-technician. He was certified to run fireworks displays and sported a sticker in the back window of his car that read "I love Explosives". Roy loved to run down anyone or anything he considered liberal. Once he labeled you, it stuck in his mind. I also remember his telling us that a castor bean plant used in making ricin, a deadly poison, grew locally nearby. This sounded a lot worse than marijuana. I reminded Roy that his explosives sticker, although related to fireworks, was not cool in an age of terrorism. I have no idea concerning the disposition of the castor beans. Last time I saw Roy, his explosives sticker was gone.

Symposia

For the next few years, I was immersed in symposia presentations with occasional teaching bouts for Adult Education. I developed a newsletter, began circulating it to local city and public service managers, converted Urban Systems Institute to a 501 (c)(3) and joined the Santee Chamber of Commerce. These newsletter contacts with city and county leaders, school officials and company managers were paying off. My growing data base of community contacts facilitated contact with the right people. Rather than announce coming events in shotgun fashion, I managed to direct my communications on specific topics to those with a special interest in that topic. This targeted approach worked and attracted those who shared a common interest in a particular topic.

Interest in the symposia was heightened by our speaker line-up – always individuals highly regarded for their expertise by their associates. The symposia, in addition to its information sharing, became a contact exchange center for professionals in the same line of work. We were at the right place at the right time with the right approach.

Participants from over 10 cities, 6 county offices, 7 special districts including San Diego Gas and Electric and the San Diego Port Authority, the Marine Corps and Navy, a number of elementary, high school and college districts plus engineering and manufacturing firms joined in these symposia. Representatives from the following organizations attended: General Atomics, Hughes Network Systems. Ketema Aerospace, Lockheed Martin, Motorola, Qualcomm, Solar Turbines, Sundstrand Aerospace, Teledyne Ryan, La Mesa-Spring Valley School District and the US Navy. Topics ranged from computer architecture, budgets, permit processing, Deming management methods and digital records to utility readings via telemetry, staff development and school innovations.

I also enjoyed the opportunity to kick-off each meeting with a summary of new books on management, announcements about coming events and the introduction of speakers. Our pro bono programs were at the same quality level as those fielded by nationally recognized consulting firms for hefty fees. But the absence of a good revenue stream was typical and our Achilles Heel

Infrastructure and High Speed Transport

Even before we activated our symposia, Bill Clinton's election and Al Gore's efforts to streamline federal operations stimulated me to develop a number of proposals. Ted Gaebler's "Reinventing Government" was having some influence in government circles at least from a talking standpoint. My proposals which dealt primarily with manpower utilization and the infrastructure were sent to elected leaders and department heads in Washington, Sacramento and locally. While these proposals got the standard "at a boy", funding didn't materialize.

Most of those proposals remain as applicable today as they were then. One had to do with redirecting the skills of engineers displaced by defense downsizing to infrastructure-related jobs. I suggested the same formula used successfully in my earlier funded program for Manpower Utilization in the seventies. But I wasn't as fortunate in the nineties as I was in the seventies. Yet every time I drive past 1600 Pacific Highway and look at the County Administration building with a 1935 construction date chiseled over the entranceway and the caption "Good Government Demands the Intelligent Interest of Every Citizen", I think of FDR's New Deal legacy. We need more legacy-conscious infrastructure renewal today especially in the high speed transport arena.

Mark and Ginny

Meanwhile, Mark and Ginny were pretty much on their own. Mark never let his epilepsy slow him down. As long as he took his medication (dilantin), his seizures were under control and few knew about his affliction. I advised Mark to keep mum on his condition if he wanted to work. Too many people would disqualify him if they knew. I realized the danger should Mark be operating dangerous equipment or diving when a seizure occurred. But as long as he took his medication, the likelihood of seizures was low. He made many boat dives off Catalina, the Channel Islands and the Caribbean. He told me that he could usually tell if a seizure was coming on by his speech - it would begin to slur. But Mark figured the odds were in his favor. He had his own tools and could drive up to any construction site and get hired. He had his ups and downs money-wise; an occupational hazard in construction work. I would help him as much as I could. But his main love, even though married twice, was his love affair with the ocean. He loved to dive solo. Scuba was part of his life. Moss Street in Laguna Beach was his favorite dive spot. No one knew the underwater coast line as well as Mark.

Other macho pursuits included parachute jumping and martial arts. His was also interested in becoming a helicopter pilot but the cost was prohibitive. But solo scuba diving remained Mark's refuge and security blanket. He was one with the sea. His primary and only real contemporary friend was Frank. I don't know where Mark met Frank but they shared the same interests – scuba, shooting and flying. Frank was a former Marine and they may have met while diving at the La Jolla Cove, a popular San Diego dive spot. After separating from the service, Frank joined an aerospace company in Florida. But the geographic distance never stopped them from getting together and doing their thing. They would exchange visits and dive and shoot either in Florida or California. In Florida, Frank, who flew his own plane, and Mark would fly to different dive spots in the Caribbean. These were probably Mark's happiest days.

Mark's marriage to Silvia was a stabilizing force in Mark's life for a short time. I had no idea how they met. She had a good job with the telephone company in Riverside and provided a stabile home environment for Mark. She was also well liked by my family. But Silvia suffered a terrible tragedy when her son drowned soon after their wedding. It seems her son along with two of his friends fell into an ice covered pond in the local mountains. All three drowned trying to rescue one another. The balloons attached to the coffins were a sad reminder of young lives cut down too soon. Not long after, Mark and Silvia divorced. I believe the cultural issue got to Mark. Mark married a second time. I didn't receive any announcement and knew nothing about the marriage until afterwards. This time his wife was a Middle Eastern girl named Ellie. She was from the Los Angeles-Ontario area. Ellie worshipped Mark but their marriage was not well received by his sisters or mother. The marriage didn't last as long as his marriage to Silvia.

Ginny was still in contact. She would take a bus to San Diego to visit me from time to time, spending a day or two with Marsha and myself, showering, washing her clothes then just as suddenly deciding she wanted to return to the Los Angeles area. Try as I might, I could never get Ginny to commit herself to the public assistance programs that would have paid for her room and board at a residential care site. She resisted any attempt to sign her up.. She was absolutely paranoid about signing anything that she perceived would limit her freedom. Meanwhile, living on the street, an inadequate diet and absence of personal grooming made her look twice her age. Her preference for wearing a hooded sweatshirt seemed to be her way of withdrawing from the world.

It broke my heart that Ginny wouldn't cooperate. It angered me that we could let people in Ginny's homeless and schizophrenic state roam the streets. "If she isn't a threat to herself or others, it's her right to roam and be homeless." That was the usual retort of social workers who kept track of street people. "We take better care of our pets than people" was my retort. Ginny would stay with us for a couple days, get some decent food into her, get her body and clothes cleaned, and then be on her way. I would see Ginny off at the Greyhound station for a trip back to her preferred haunt, Santa Monica. Marsha was always relieved when Ginny left because Ginny smoked and Marsha was always afraid that if left alone she would burn the house down.

Charlotte and Robin

Charlotte was my pride and joy. When she decided she was going to do something, she did it. She established career and educational goals that assured her independence and self-sufficiency. I'm sure Charlotte could have become a medical doctor but she chose nursing, took a master's degree in the field, became a family nurse practitioner, opened her own clinic, married a doctor and gave me three beautiful grandchildren, all girls. Charlotte was always a goal-oriented, busy girl, well-liked and a natural leader. She was partial to her brother Mark, did what she could to help

Robin when Robin was on the skids from drugs and alcohol. Like myself, Charlotte felt frustrated at not being able to do more to help Ginny.

Occasionally, Robin, my youngest, would drop by with her new boyfriend. Her recent divorce from Steve, like so many divorces, tore their lives apart. Divorce always takes a toll, especially on kids. In this case, my granddaughter Amber got caught up in a shared custody arrangement. The divorce cost Robin and Steve their new home in Pacifica. Robin continued working as an office manager and rented an apartment in a San Francisco suburb. I'm not sure how she met Robert, her new companion, but he was into sailing and Robin plunged into the world of boating. She would maintain a boating interest until her untimely death.

Teamwork, Technology and Learning

Meanwhile, our symposia work was taking on another dimension – an actual on-campus program for middle school youth. We referred to this program as TTL or Teamwork, Technology and Learning. This was an almost spontaneous outgrowth of our management and educational symposia which brought together some highly regarded community leaders willing to break with paradigms of the past. Moving from ingrained methods to something new is not easy. Strong leaders can be change agents as long as they remain at the helm. But old habits readily creep back in if change does not become imbedded and, over time, part of the business culture. Modifying behavior for the long term is not easy. One behavioral change we sought to make was teamwork. We wanted to see more collaboration in the workplace and in the schools. While reviewing some of the details of the new program with Frank Nakamura in the LaMesa YMCA locker room, a counselor named Roger from nearby Parkway Middle School overheard our conversation and invited us to present our program to his school principal, Frank Murphy. Roger said his boss was open to innovative ideas. Thanks to Frank Murphy and Roger's support, information about our program got out to the parents. As a result, we were able to put together a select group of some thirty students. Our only restriction was that our program must not interfere with the regular school day. So we scheduled our program a class period before the regular school day began. Parents would have to get the kids to school without the regular bus service. And they did.

This was a time when parents were looking for any advantage they could get when it came to the education of their children. Changes stemming from "A Nation at Risk" report of the early eighties and America 2000 were beginning to find their way into schools. Charter school legislation was emerging and charter schools were coming on line. Parents were as sensitive to the need for improving our public schools as was the business community. So the enrichment opportunity of our TTL program appealed to parents. We even invited the parents to attend the classes and many did.

The essence of our TTL program was its teamwork. Our thirty students were grouped into six project groups of five students each. The assignment for each group was to create a new business. Their project activity was buttressed by representatives from a variety of local business enterprises. A representative from a different enterprise like engineering, manufacturing, telecom, banking and government described how knowledge was shared and how teamwork got the job done in each enterprise. The students were then challenged to do likewise with an undertaking of their own creation.

Meanwhile, with input from these leaders and guidance from Frank and Harry, the students immersed themselves in their team projects. Each team member assumed responsibility for a distinct element whether it be design, manufacturing, marketing, finance or facilities. Each team developed a presentation designed to convince a banker that putting up the necessary capital was a sound investment. This was an exercise in management fundamentals. A similar approach would later carry over into the design of a special summer school program and charter school.

The community's participation in these activities was excellent. A morning schedule that began earlier than the regular school day worked to our advantage. Except for a field trip, interference with the regular school day was minimal. Our standout field experience involved a tour of Sundstrand Aerospace. The kids got to see a real enterprise in operation, meet the management and workers and saw first-hand how a company teamed up to make their finished product. The local newspaper covered the events and the kids enjoyed the publicity. They even made some suggestions to the hosting company for streamlining certain company operations. For its work in producing this program, Urban Systems was awarded a small grant by the Sundstrand Corporation.

Portugal, Spain, Morocco, Gibraltar and Cancun

It was vacation time again. This time, thanks to Marsha's time share, we were able to book accommodations in Portugal and Spain. About a year or so earlier, we used Marsha's time share to vacation in Cancun where we snorkeled among exotically colored fish at Cozumel and visited the Mayan ruins at Tulum and Chichen Itza. I was really impressed with the pyramids and playing courts at Chichen Itza. It has never ceased to amaze me how a society of such capable architects, astrologists and mathematicians could disappear so suddenly. Once again, I returned with hours of video that I would share with students in future classes.

My fondness for Portugal has to do with my admiration of Prince Henry the Navigator and the school of nautical knowledge he put together. He was a staunch promoter of expeditions and mapping. He was one of the first to use the Caravel, the fastest and most maneuverable ship of the day. One of the souvenirs that attracted me in Lagos was a small ceramic coaster bearing the imprint of a Caravel. I bought several and gave one to each member of our charter-organizing group. It represented our solidarity and our venture into new waters.

Although we didn't get to many of the sights in mainland Spain, my memory of driving on with endless fields of sunflower plants in full bloom on each side remains vivid. I was also impressed by the calmness of the Mediterranean Sea as we sailed from Spain to Morocco then back to Gibraltar. It was like sailing on a big lake.

Marsha and Fibromyalgia

Marsha managed to hold up on all our trips despite the aches and pains of fibromyalgia. At that time, opinions in the medical community on how to handle fibromyalgia were split. Some doctors thought the pain was psychological rather than physical. But the pain was real. She winced even whenever I touched her. I marveled at her fortitude in getting up each day and going to work as a bookkeeper for a sailing supply company in Point Loma. Occasionally, she attended some meetings of fibromyalgia support groups to learn from others what they were doing to reduce the pain. Eventually she found the medication that reduced the pain. After years of dismissing fibromyalgia pain as an imaginary ailment, the medical community finally got around to recognizing it as a very real and painful ailment.

Pre-charter Pilot

Charter school activity had been picking up across the nation. Legislators were creating the legislation necessary to unshackle barriers to school innovation. It was a movement driven by complaints from parents and the business community alike that the regular public school system was not getting the job done. When someone suggested we move in that direction, I balked. It seemed to me we had more than we could handle trying to influence change from the inside. But we decided to test the educational approach we had already demonstrated at the La Mesa-Spring Valley school district in Santee. This would extend our reach and influence. We approached Marcia Johnson, the Santee School District superintendent, and presented our demonstration proposal.

I believe Marcia was favorably disposed to our proposal because of our previous successful experience with innovation and the qualifications of our group. As superintendent, she walked a cautious line between the teacher union and the school board. But our planning group which by now had expanded to include a couple retired educators and engineers was impressive. Marcis's father was a former engineer at General Dynamics and she had fond memories of helping him as a child on projects around the house. She was level headed and didn't leave things to chance.

Marcia put us through the hoops in terms of defining our goals, target group and innovations. We had to submit an acceptable lesson plan to her and her Assistant Superintendent for Instruction. But the background of our team coupled with high recommendations from the La Mesa – Spring Valley bolstered her confidence in giving us the green light. Our management symposia and a recently completed forum on educational philosophies and teaching methods also bolstered our standing in the community. As usual, our education-related discussions were anchored in the work of education notables such as Horace Mann, John Dewey, Robert Hutchinson, Mortimer Adler and Allan Bloom.

Adler's books on reforming education, how to speak, how to listen, how to read a book and the Paideia Proposal had significant influence on me. In his Paideia proposal, Adler defines the teacher as a gardener responsible for nurturing and guiding the knowledge growth of his students. It is the teacher's responsibility to create an environment supportive of the student's potential. This concept as well as Adler's insistence that source documents be used in the learning process helped shape the design of our future charter school.

I put together a lesson plan for a four week summer program that would engage an evenly divided gender mix of 6-7-8th graders. The program provided an overview of the key events associated with the nation's founding such as the founding fathers, key documents of the Revolution including Thomas Paine's Common Sense, the Declaration of Independence, the Federalist Papers and even the post-revolutionary work of Alexis DeTocqueville's "Democracy in America". Local, state and federal officials plus representatives from military and civic organizations made an appearance..I even had my cousins, Jack and Bobbie O'Donnell, both retirees from the US Postal Service, describe the evolution of the Post Office. The highlight of the program, however, was the field trip to the Marine Corps Recruit Depot in downtown San Diego adjacent Lindbergh Field. The Santee Kiwanis Club made the bus trip possible by underwriting its costs. Retired Marine Sergeant Major Bill Paxton, an active member of the Santee Kiwanis, was instrumental in securing Kiwanis support. Bill, whose father was lost during the battle for Iwo Jima, was usually the center of many local activities involving the Corps. Later, he would help us get our charter school off the ground. The trip to MCRD to view newly minted Marines marching to the base band and a tour of the command museum made a fitting capstone for our program.

Although these were very busy days, the dancing respite in the evening went a long way towards keeping the body in shape and the spirits high.

Charter school Formation

Soon after completion of our summer program, our work to develop a new charter school went into high gear. This meant talking to the Santee PTA, the local Chamber and service clubs and setting up petition signature booths the entrance to leading shopping centers. It meant attending all the charter school related meetings held regularly at the main San Diego Chamber of Commerce offices in downtown San Diego.. John Walton, a member of the WalMart family, lived in National City and underwrote the Chamber costs for these monthly meetings. The Walton family was a staunch supporter of charter schools.

The Chamber meetings provided existing charter operators and those preparing to start a charter school a convenient center for keeping abreast of all charter-related information. There were reports on success stories and problem areas, heads-up regarding legislative action or anticipated committee action in the Assembly or Senate Education committees, interpretation of disputed areas within the charter law and issues ranging from direct payment to charters and the composition of charter school boards.

Charter schools were new and growing but resistance was mounting. School districts were extremely sensitive to the loss of revenue due to student transfers to a charter school. At the same time, there was a cap on charters. In those early days, the cap on charter schools state-wide stood at 100 and charters were approaching their cap. San Diego Unified was sponsoring several charters including High Tech High while Grossmont Union was sponsoring Helix High and Lakeside the Riverdale middle school.

I invited Marcia Johnson, the Santee School District superintendent, to attend one of the meetings and she did. She was one of the few if not the first superintendent from the mainstream to attend a charter meeting. This gave her an opportunity to meet the drivers of the movement in San Diego - leaders like Ginger Hovenic whose organizational skills helped steer and encourage the expansion of charters in San Diego. Other charter leaders who regularly attended these meetings included Ted Smith, principal of Helix High, Mary Bixby from the store-front schools, Coach Snyder from Escondido and Brian Williams whose penetrating legislative analysis kept us abreast of charter developments in Sacramento.

Meanwhile back in Santee, more and more parents were signing up for our charter school. They liked our philosophy, our approach and dress code. We adopted Jimmy's Restaurant in Santee as our regular meeting venueand designated Saturday mornings as our meeting time. Jimmy's had an ideal meeting room for groups such as ours. We combined our meeting with breakfast. A growing number of parents were participating and Saturday mornings at Jimmy's was the ideal place to keep abreast. I estimated we would need an enrollment of at least a hundred students to get our school off the ground. It was easy to do the revenue math because the State allowed a fixed amount for students at different grade levels. Daily attendance reports were the basis for the State's Average Daily Attendance (ADA) calculation, the basis for school funding. We would focus on middle school grades 6th,7th and 8th initially then, as our school stabilized, we would seek authorization to extend our grade levels through the 12th grade.

Charters, however, did not have all the expenses their public school counterparts had covered. Expenses for transportation and school housing were not covered. You could only avoid the school housing expense if your charter school was a conversion of an entire public school to a charter status. Most charters, however, were not that lucky and school districts weren't inclined to make space available even if it existed. Charter schools were viewed as competitors and threats to their revenue streams. A good example of an entire high school converting to charter status is Helix High, part of the Grossmont Unified School District. Santee is a good example of a school district having space that might have been made available for a small charter but unwilling to make that space be available despite legislation requiring districts to share space if available. There was always some excuse for non-availability like a need for storage space or, better yet, need for income by selling it. Santee did exactly this in putting unused classroom space out of reach for our charter and, later, with sell-off of an entire school and its grounds due to declining enrollment.

Most charters had to find their own facilities. This meant a heavy monthly outlay for leasing. Next to salaries, leasing costs consumed the bulk of the budget. Plus, there was the challenge of ensuring that facilities met safety, fire, zoning and environmental requirements. Acquiring code-compliant facilities, especially where a school is involved, is a demanding task.

Parents were eager to get their kids into a smaller school setting where methods, a dress code and the absence of drugs and bullying would provide a better learning environment. The Santee teacher association president questioned the need for a charter school. In her opinion, the Santee School District was doing fine. Why didn't we set up a charter school in neighborhoods like Logan Heights or other communities where performance levels were lower? Wasn't that the intent of the charter school legislation? Besides, why should men in their seventies want to get involved with school affairs? Why not just retire, sit on the sidelines and watch the world go by?

I was pretty blunt in answering these questions. I made it clear that we were taking on a much overlooked segment of students who were caught in a learning environment detrimental to better academic performance and whose teaching methods afforded no choice for parents. The only choice most parents had was a private school and private schooling was beyond the financial reach of most. It was our contention that lacking a choice of learning methods and suitable learning environment, too many students were not realizing their potential. Too many students were simply coasting through. Targeting an unchallenged segment of the school population would offer parents a chance to put their children in an environment designed to motivate and improve their performance.

Until charters came along, the parents had little choice in school selection. Most could not afford a private school and most expected the local public school to turn out capable graduates. However, due to the criticism of the business community and parents that too many graduates were ill-prepared for the world awaiting them, a charter school movement emerged designed to offer parents a choice while providing a competitive model for the standard public school system. Charters provide choice. We wanted parents, even in white, middle class Santee, to have a choice in choosing a public school that was smaller and more effective.

Stand-patters argued that a middle class city like Santee with a low minority presence did not fit the typical charter profile and that Santee parents neither wanted nor needed a school option. The parents who signed up for the charter disagreed. Choice of a smaller, more wholesome and uniformed learning environment was exactly what the parents wanted. As sign-ups continued to grow, we began our search for a school site. Most of the parents signing up lived in Santee making that locale a natural especially since funds for a bus service were not part of the charter budget. As we would soon learn, getting a suitable facility for a school is easier said than done. And, before you can commit to a school start date, you must, in addition to faculty, have a suitable location established.

Looking back, the nineties with all its school-oriented activities culminated with a charter plan whose promise would be prematurely cut short because of facility issues.

Chapter 8

FIRST DECADE – 21ˢᵗ CENTURY

The momentous events of the first decade of a new century set the stage for unprecedented challenges. All of us were caught up in a swirl of national and international events that have been shaping our future since. We were witness to a Supreme Court decision that gave the Florida vote and presidency to George W. Bush, the 9/11 terrorist attack on the New York Twin Towers with a loss of life exceeding that of Pearl Harbor, a plane crash into the Pentagon and a valiant sacrifice by passengers of United Flight 93, an invasion of Iraq, the toppling of Saddam Hussein, an invasion of Afghanistan in pursuit of Bin Laden, Hurricane Katrina and the New Orleans disaster, the Haitian earthquake, the Gulf oil spill and its impact on the Gulf States, the Mexican drug wars, the nuclear threat of North Korea and Iran, the continuing Palestinian-Israeli conflict, the Enron and Wall Street scandals, the mortgage industry collapse, the election of Barak Obama, the auto industry bail-outs, stimulus funding, unemployment levels unheard of since the Great Depression and Europe struggling to forestall a collapse of their own.

The Charter School

After our charter goals, methods and performance expectations were reduced to writing, we gathered the required parent signatures and submitted our charter school petition to the Santee School Board. Legislation governing charter school formation spelled out the timelines for Board action so approval came quickly. Our Santee Explorer Academy charter was forwarded to Sacramento and approved. Meantime we submitted an application to the State for a loan to get the school off and running. It too was forthcoming quickly. But that was a mistake. Never go for a loan. Go for a grant. A loan can hang over a charter school like a Damocles sword

We received a loan from the State for $250,000 making it possible to acquire facilities, equip the school and open our doors by our September target date. Another big mistake. Use grant money not loans and don't open a school until all the basic staffing, supplies and equipment are fully in place. And, never open a school until potential pitfalls surrounding a lease are identified and addressed.

Finally, make sure that all purchases and expenditures, beginning with day one, are receipted and that auditable bookkeeping practices are in place.

We had a lot of unscrambling to do after the rush to open left us with a lot of receipts accumulated in the proverbial shoebox. To make matters worse, the individual designated as our financial officer resigned from the position.

School financial accounting can seem arcane to those unfamiliar with public school financing. Keeping on top of attendance reporting, payment schedules from the State, property tax allocations from the County Assessor, lottery receipts, grant dollars, interest-bearing accounts and payroll requires experience or a very quick learning ability. Confidence in one's accounting system is essential and it must be in place beginning with the first school day. Fortunately, the California Charter School Association and the fiscal divisions of the County Superintendent were quick to realize that school accounting could be a charter school's Achilles Heel. The County Ed department established a training program for school finance directors and began regular monthly meetings. But our loss of a Financial Director in the school's first month of operation threw us a curve. Fortunately, this challenge was overcome when I recruited a long time friend from former aerospace days – Bob Mendoza. Bob had a background in finance and accounting. His support was invaluable. He pulled our bacon out of the fire.

Bob Mendoza

Bob was the best story-tellers I ever knew. I don't know whether it was a Spanish inflection in his English, the glint in his eye, the cadence of his speech or just his knack for recounting events in an entertaining manner. He was a very popular guy. I can't imagine him ever having an enemy. He was also very good with numbers and a real stickler for getting it right – especially where money was concerned. We knew one another from our earlier days of working for General Dynamics in its Management and Information Systems group.

I still remember Bob's story about bumping into General MacArthur in a stairwell while stationed in Japan just after the war. Bob was holding an ice cream cone in one hand and papers in the other as he was descending a stairwell when General MacArthur was coming up. To hear Bob tell his story about his saluting dilemma was really funny. Apparently MacArthur recognized Bob's dilemma and smiled. But Bob had many other stories. One he particularly liked was the story of his youthful poverty in Arizona and how his memories of an empty refrigerator kept him motivated to this day to keep a full refrigerator. But Bob had a talent for financial affairs. He unscrambled the jumble of receipts and invoices accumulated during our opening days. Bob put our financial house in order.

Staffing

The quality of your staffing makes or breaks your school. Originally, I thought that at least part of our teaching staff could be recruited from the ranks of retired teachers or professionals. The underlying assumption was that such individuals were experienced, stabile, had medical insurance, had family obligations behind them, would find our class schedules less taxing physically and provide additional income. Unfortunately, I struck out here. When our initial recruiting was over, our teacher profile was much younger and equally divided between men and women.

Although the ranks of seniors who would prefer to remain active and pursue new adventures is growing, the happenstance of a Frank

Nakamura, Harry Vorrath, Bob Mendoza and a Bob Byron converging at the same place, at the same time with a common interest is rare. Yet, it seems history is replete with things happening because the right combination of people come together at the right time at the right place. The happenstance of our coming together, all of us in an age bracket that conventional wisdom would have slotted into the retirement column, was proof that innovation and leadership are not the exclusive preserve of youth. Our dreams and ambitions kept us as young as people half our age.

One of my favorite philosophers, Viktor Frankl defines happiness as the feeling of fulfillment derived from satisfying and meaningful work. During the time we worked together, we were the happy few.

Gillespie Field and Innovations

Our school stood apart from others on several counts. Part of our facilities was located at Gillespie Field, a county airport complete with flying schools, two air museums and facilities for business jets. One museum was privately owned and housed WWI era aircraft. Another was an annex to the Balboa Park Air and Space museum. This museum housed post WWII jets plus a machine shop for rebuilding damaged aircraft, a shop for building model airplanes and a classroom. Outside the Air and Space museum annex facility an Atlas missile was on exhibit along with several vintage jets. Our administrative offices were housed in a separate building at the airport and we also rented an additional hangar for classroom space. Our ultimate goal was to have some of our students qualify for pilot licenses before they graduated. Other classrooms were rented at a shopping center bordering the airfield. The airfield was in El Cajon. The shopping center was in Santee.

A stock car race track and a soccer field also bordered Gillespie Field. We leased the soccer field for sports and recreational activities. This site was also used as our kick-off point on opening day. Parents, students and staff convened here and I gave a brief welcoming talk. It was one of the proudest moments of my life. We then proceeded to our classrooms in the adjoining shopping center. School was now in session.

The organization of the curricula would undergo adjustments before a routine set in. There were several things we wanted to accomplish. One was faculty teamwork and the actual blending of knowledge from different disciplines. The other was a class schedule that would facilitate this integration of knowledge. Related subjects were clustered so that teachers could more readily correlate the content of one subject to another. For example, over a one month period, the focus might be on biology, chemistry and physics. During another month, the focus would be on history, government and English. We used team projects to showcase the students' ability to blend knowledge from different disciplines into their presentations. For subjects requiring repetitive actions for proficiency, like computer software and a foreign language, a daily schedule was in place. Teachers not scheduled to teach in a given month were on-call to support on-duty teachers on field trips and student coaching.

Field trips were an important part of our learning process and used as extensively as our budget allowed. We also put the musical talent of some of our teachers at the disposal of our students whenever we could. For physical education, we used our soccer field and the services of a local martial arts instructor. The martial arts program was not only a good physical conditioner and laboratory for demonstrating principles of physics but also a motivator for self-discipline.

One of our most challenging issues involved the reading level of our students. While a 6th, 7th and 8th grade reading level was expected, our entry tests indicated that more than half our students were reading below grade level. In addition, the number of Special Ed students admitted exceeded the average ratio. Fortunately, through the efforts of a very talented teacher, all students in the Special Ed category were mainstreamed into regular activities and their individual educational programs discontinued.

There were some unanticipated bumps in the road at the beginning in addition to our facility challenges.. Screen as we might, a couple of our staff had their own agenda including forming a charter of their own or using the school as a springboard to alter our primary target group. At a meeting convened for our parents, staff and sponsor, I had an opportunity to restate our mission as defined in our state-approved charter and suggested that those found our approach not a match for their expectations should reconsider their choice. The presentation cleared the air. We lost a couple of students.

But the thing that hurt us more than anything else was loss of our classrooms at the shopping center just across the street from the airfield. That setback was a result of the Sheriff informing us of a law prohibiting student classrooms in the vicinity of shooting range. I knew a shooting range was nearby. In fact, I had even planned to take advantage of the fact to introduce our upperclassmen to safety requirements in gun handling. But I wasn't aware of any law excluding schools from centers where shooters would be walking from a parking lot to a range carrying their guns.

We then attempted to rent open space near the airfield for portable classrooms only to be informed that an endangered plant grew in the area and the State prohibited any building in the area. Without any other affordable, code compliant facilities nearby, we accepted an offer to rent classroom space on the premises of the Home of the Guiding Hand on the east side of Santee.

Home of the Guiding Hands

Some parents objected to having their children schooled on a site that housed the developmentally disabled. This cost us some students. However, the layout of classrooms in the building was such that they ringed an administrative hub in the center. It was ideal for communication and oversight. The outdoor recreational facilities were also ideal for ball games, track and martial arts. But the move meant relinquishing our soccer field, our classroom in the Air and Space museum annex and the whole ambiance of the airfield stimulation.

While at the Home of the Guiding Hands, a fatal shooting took place at Santana High School just a few blocks away from our school. A 15 year old had opened fire on the school campus killing 2 and wounding 13. It was reminiscent of the Columbine school shooting in Colorado two years earlier when 13 were killed and over 20 injured. I was off-campus when I first heard the report over the radio. I hurried back to school and convened staff and students. I wanted to calm fears and enlist support in preventing such an occurrence on our campus. I told the staff and students we would all have to be more sensitive to the talk and behavior of those around us. Where repeated speech or action patterns indicated distress, depression or anger, we would have to make help and counseling available as soon as possible. Earlier we had a prank incident involving chemicals that might have caused injury. Disciplinary action was taken. But sometimes, even disciplinary action can trigger additional violence. I experienced a gun threat after expelling a student for his continuous disruptive behavior. Fortunately, such threats are rare.

But our days at the Home of the Guiding Hand were numbered. After several months of occupancy, the Directors of the Home of the Guiding Hands determined that they could not renew our rental agreement because their by-laws required them to use their resources exclusively in support of the developmentally disabled.

Church in El Cajon

Once again, our search for facilities was on. This time the property selection had narrowed down to a church that had several classrooms not being used during the week. A church property was far from my first choice. But available facilities that were up to code and affordable were few and far between. We were between a rock and a hard place. We needed the classrooms and the church needed the income. So our new school now moved further from Santee. The church property was located in a neighboring city, El Cajon.

Establishing a public school on church property has its drawbacks. One drawback is a natural perception that the school is affiliated with a particular religion and not a public school. This perception has diminished or scotched the use of vouchers by public school students for private school attendance at sites where a religious orientation could be presumed. In a 2002 US Supreme Court ruling in Zelman v Simmons-Harris, the court held 5-4 that voucher use for schooling in private sectarian environment does not conflict with US Constitution provided the funds are not used to promote a religion and attendees are not required to attend or participate in religion-oriented services. About ten states now authorize the use of vouchers but such usage, when put before the voters, is usually voted down. Even though many schools with a religious orientation have reputations for academic excellence, the establishment clause of the First Amendment is interpreted as a barrier to the co-mingling public funds in a sectarian environment.

The classrooms, auditorium and outdoor facilities at El Cajon were adequate facility-wise but the travel distance to the new location was inconvenient for some parents and, again, we lost some students.

In our first month of operation in our rented church facilities, the startling and tragic experience of 9/11 took place. As we met in general assembly on that fateful morning, confusing reports of what had happened were just starting to come in. Two airliners had crashed into the Twin Towers in New York. Casualty projections were just coming in. Within the next day or so we would learn that the loss of life exceeded that of Pearl Harbor and that a terrorist organization called Al Queda headed by Ben Ladin was responsible. The whole mood of the country changed on that fateful day. We were united and focused on bringing those responsible to justice. Patriotism surged.

Meanwhile, our facility instability was proving to be our Achilles Heel. We moved three times in little over a year. Academically we were doing fine despite the moves. Our teachers were performing well and student test scores were up. Thanks to a grant, we had a good computer lab with Internet connection. Parents were pleased with the academic progress of the students.

School Closing

We were about to launch a new recruiting campaign for students in the El Cajon area when a professor from a local community college approached me with an unique suggestion. He proposed that our school include a component for adults seeking a regular high school diploma. The adults he had in mind were those living in half-way houses and under court order to attend school. Many lacked a high school diploma and preferred a diploma from a regular high school as opposed to a GED (general education development) certification. There were enough adults available for enrollment to overcome our revenue shortfall. Classes would be held at their halfway house facilities so there would be no intermingling of students and no cost to us for use of their facilities. But the sponsoring school board didn't see it that way. The school board didn't like the proposed adult component and didn't like our present location outside the district boundaries. They saw our student loss at each move as putting us as on a glide path to fiscal unsustainability. The Santee School board withdrew their sponsorship. We were out of business.

We turned all our new computer equipment over to the Santee district. Whatever equipment the district did not want was auctioned off. We closed our accounting books and were given a clean bill of health by an independent auditing firm. That we did as well as we did on a shoestring is a tribute to Bob Mendoza's yeoman efforts.

What hurt me more than anything was seeing our parents and their kids having to transfer to other schools. I had other charter operators in the area make presentations about their schools to the parents. But most charters had waiting lists and were limited by their facility size. The average size of most charters is about 600 students. The smaller student body is easier to manage and enhances student-teacher interaction. Several mainstream public schools, in an effort to achieve the academic results of charters, have developed mini schools within their campuses. This emulation of charters is one of the anticipated by-products of the charter legislation.

Like anyone else, I hated the idea of losing a school. I wanted to see at least one graduating class. To me, nothing was so heart-wrenching as to see students return to schools they were so glad to leave earlier. I remember the taunting words of the Santee superintendent when she told me it was not likely I'd get support for another charter. But I wasn't ready to throw in the towel. I knew it was only a matter of time before

I would re-engage in comparable or related activities. It's in my blood. It is what I do. So I went back to the drawing boards.

Lessons Learned

My experience and observation of charter schools led me to certain conclusions regarding capital for a school start-up and progressive development. First, I would never take borrowed money for start-up capital. The State does provide grants, usually on a competitive basis. This is the recommended route for financing. Second, facilities must be adequate, affordable, reasonably permanent and large enough to accommodate the school's planned expansion. Third, each student should have an Internet connected laptop, desktop or tablet and the classroom equipped with document camera, smart board and white board. Teachers should be prepared to adopt the latest learning technology as it becomes available.

Bernie's Passing

Meanwhile a series of tragedies began to unfold during this decade. Bernie, who had suffered for years from an undetected problem, succumbed to cancer. I was with her in her final moments and was able to tell her I always loved her. I think there is something about a first love that is immutable. In the final years of our marriage, Bernie used to say she loved me but didn't like me. Maybe being liked is better. Maybe there is too much pain when love is involved. As much as I loved family and friends, I was never very effusive in verbally expressing it. I felt actions spoke louder than words. I envisioned my role as an economic mainstay even though I had my share of economic ups and downs. I always felt it was the wife's role to provide a stable love and affection platform for the family. Bernie and I were not on the same page when it came to sex or expressing our feelings and needs. All the women I've ever known were much better than I when it came to verbalizing feelings. I think I put too much stock in the belief that actions spoke louder than words. I think women need words as much as actions. But Bernie was my first and truest love. Never since have I felt so deep a love and commitment as I had for Bernie. I whispered that in her ear in her final moments.

Charlotte managed the funeral arrangements. Bernie was cremated. We took her ashes to San Pedro where we boarded a boat, took out to sea, and sprinkled her ashes over the Pacific. Mark delivered a stirring and heartfelt eulogy. I didn't expect such eloquence.

Classroom Revisited

After the closing the school, I was back in the classroom in short order. I resumed my World Affairs and US History programs as a faculty adjunct for Palomar College and conducted a special seminar series for middle managers from China's Guandong Province at Southwestern College. I also became a visiting professor for the Osher and Oasis Foundations and a visiting teacher for several school districts including Grossmont, Sweetwater and San Diego Unified. When Palomar discontinued its outreach programs, I continued holding classes for my former students at the Escondido Redwood Town Center at their request on an independent basis.

It is hard to say which student groups I prefer. I enjoy the freshness and hopefulness of middle and high school students. I enjoy the challenge of adult groups especially where the reading, educational and experience levels are high. These groups kept me on my toes. I learn as much from them as they do from me. In fact, the secret to the success of these classes lies in creating a climate for constructive discussion where opinion is divided on sensitive issues. There is a real need for more classes of this nature. Too many Americans are held captive to the same talking heads on TV or radio and, except for occasional town hall meetings with elected representatives, seldom get the opportunity to express their own views in a public forum. There are few opportunities for civil discourse in open forum where opinions vary. Classes that tackle thorny issues provide a welcome outlet for adults who want to be heard and are willing to interact with others.

Osher, Oasis and Great Decisions

Osher Foundation courses take place on university campuses throughout the country. In San Diego their programs are conducted at CSU-San Marcos, UC San Diego and San Diego State University.

On campus facilities are ideal especially those at San Diego State where there are dedicated classrooms facilities and convenient parking. Oasis, on the other hand, uses facilities provided by Macy's right on the store's premises. The mall at which the Macy's store is located provides convenient parking for Oasis attendees.

I've always enjoyed the challenge of designing courses that required a little more in-depth reading and interest in biographical materials on presidents or other prominent figures. I usually focus on creating a discussion environment for the many national priorities that divide us. Recently I began correlating the content of the Foreign Policy Association's Great Decisions program into my World Affairs program since both address similar issues. The Great Decisions program highlights six topics a year, topics that usually coincide with my material. How the Great Decisions program escaped my attention over the years is beyond me. But I conducted the program at Osher's request for a group of retired professionals resident in a posh retirement center in La Jolla. Much of the Great Decisions program content is integral to the material covered in my World Affairs program to this day.

I also approached the chair of San Diego State's Political Science department, my old alma mater, to determine if there would be any interest in incorporating the program in their graduate seminars in International Relations. To my delight, I found that the university had a World Affairs Institute. The professor in charge even contributed to the Great Decisions' annual handbook. The meeting brought back memories of my own student days there some fifty years earlier when Minos Generales, my former Political Science professor, led a similar Institute.

Minos was a polished lawyer and an expert on Middle East affairs. I remember being in one of his graduate seminars entitled "Crisis in the Middle East". Within that small group, there were two exchange students - Saed Darkanzali from Syria and Israel Dubner from Israel. The Palestine-Israeli conflict and Middle Eastern oil were at the heart of the discussion. Saed and Israel embodied the conflict more vividly than any book. I remember the seminar taking place during Ramadan and Saed anxiously awaiting sundown so he could eat. Saed was personable and we became friends. He met my family and introduced us to Garbanzo beans and Tahini sauce. He also had his family in Syria send me a beautiful, gold trimmed, sheik outfit complete with headgear. I've used that authentic Arab garb over the years on many occasions including Hallowe'en. My gift to Saed was a camera I had purchased in Japan.

Some of the Osher and Oasis courses are of a "break the mold" nature in terms of content and scope. The Adler advocacy of using source documents shone through on many of my programs. One such course involved the examination of early colonial documents related to the governance of the original colonies. An analysis of documents such as Common Sense, the Declaration of Independence, the Federalist Papers, the Constitution, and DeTocqueville's Democracy in America provides exceptional learning depth to the understanding of the American mindset in the formative years. Yale University is a repository of many historical documents and most have been reduced to a digital format. When these documents are projected on a large screen, a review of the actual text provides an excellent discussion stimulant.

Another course involved a comparative analysis of political party platforms and the philosophies and issues underlying party differences. Courses like these are rare finds within college catalogs. Courses of this nature are generally reserved for graduate level seminars. But many Osher and Oasis students have arrived at a point in their lives where the philosophic underpinning of the nation's value system can be discussed dispassionately. A review of the causes and effects of societies throwing off the yolk of old in terms of governance and economics assumes increasing importance. Where the foment for change is strongest, a prior history of democratic institutions is weakest. What appears to be an almost spontaneous rise in opposing the status quo reflects dissatisfaction with a government and institutions incapable of meeting the most basic needs. An exceptionally prescient work addressing the phenomenon of change is Alvin and Heidi Toffler's 1994 book entitled "Creating a New Civilization". It should be required reading.

China Delegation

For the past several years, Southwestern College has been hosting a management program for a select group of mid-level public officials from China. It was my privilege to lead such a course in 2003 in conjunction with the city of Chula Vista.

San Diego has a special appeal to the Chinese because of its size, coastal location, high tech industry and weather - all comparable to Guandong province. Guandong is located on China's southeastern seacoast. Hong Kong sits directly offshore at the same parallel. The Guangzhou metropolis is a showcase for China's industry and modernization.

The management course provided a comprehensive overview of our local government operations including privatization efforts and the role of unions. Many managers from a variety of public functions in Guangdong province participate as do counterpart public managers in San Diego. This arrangement contributes significantly to the credibility and timeliness of the program.

The Chinese participants were young and enthusiastic. Their English was good although it was the first course I ever taught where I was advised to speak slowly and avoid the use of idiomatic expressions that might confuse the Chinese participants. The program's founder and department chair was Viara Giraffe. She, had visited Guandong on several occasions and was impressed with the Chinese ability to deliver on its promises. When Chinese officials would tell her that upon her return next year a new factory would be standing at a designated spot, she would return to find that factory completed and operating right on time.

The delegation had a keen interest in the privatization of governmental functions. This made introduction of the book Reinventing Government by Gaebler and Osborn a natural. They were also interested in public employee unions and how effective the unions were in improving worker pay and benefits. Even WalMart, traditionally opposed to unions, had to accept union representation to operate their stores in China.

We capped the China Advanced Studies group program with a farewell party on the sand at Crown Point in the Mission Beach area. I was presented with a signed class picture inscribed with a note of appreciation.

Cruise Liners

There were also proposals to establish a lecture series aboard local cruise liners to explore the history and socio-economics of the countries serving as ports of call. The cruise liner school went nowhere. Such learning cruises seem better suited to college students getting credit for the classes. Although the idea of a school at sea is tried and true, the operation is expensive. Some years ago Chapman College in Orange County operated such a ship until operating costs made it prohibitive. But shipboard travel is an excellent way to sow the seeds of international cooperation and understanding. The Navy appreciates this fact and operates a very robust program of international travel for its Annapolis Midshipmen.

Midway Carrier Museum

I always felt the Midway carrier museum, anchored just off Harbor Drive in San Diego bay, had great potential for a small charter school. A carrier charter school would make up for the benefits lost when we had to relocate from Gillespie Airfield after less than a year operating at that location. The carrier would provide an opportunity for an up-close acquaintance with the skills and technology applications to be found aboard a carrier. A carrier is a floating city and an airfield. Every imaginable skill or technology lies within its confines. Volunteers aboard the Midway, most of whom are retired military, serve as docents. The students, once versed in carrier operations, could even assist as tour guides and perform certain shipboard duties. This site would also stimulate interest in a military career especially in the Navy or Marine Corps. Proximity to Naval and Marine facilities and retired docents would offer a superlative environment for middle and senior high school students.

The Midway board of directors declined our request to establish a charter school aboard the carrier when it first docked here. However, the museum has become a powerful educational force within the community. It regularly hosts tours for students in San Diego schools. I still think, however, that the Midway would be an ideal site for a small charter school to conduct one year of its schooling aboard the Midway. A class of some 30-40 students would pose little interference with the carrier's operations. Charter school staff and students would even also be an additional source of volunteer support.

For any new charter school, it is recommended the school begin at one grade level and expand its grade levels one year at a time until the 12th grade is reached. In San Diego with its heavy military population, a small, charter school might even be operated on military premises. A uniform dress code would apply.

Marine Historical Society Membership

About this time I joined the MCRD Historical Society which maintains the most comprehensive Marine museum west of the Mississippi. The museum houses a remarkable collection of arms, uniforms, photos, maps, art work and archives. It is open to the public during regular business hours.

The Historical Society also hosts a quarterly awards breakfast at which time leading Marine Drill Instructors are presented awards for outstanding service. These breakfast meetings also feature guest speakers who keep Historical Society members abreast of the latest information on budgets, training techniques, troop strength, new construction and policies affecting current and future missions.

Barbara McCurtis, the Museum Director, and Chuck Archuleta, the Exhibits Specialist, have made the museum a showpiece of Marine Corps history and an ideal site for special events. Angie Salinas, MCRD's Commanding one star, now a two star and recently retired, was the MCRD commanding general from 2006-2009. During her tenure at MCRD, the Museum expanded and made giant strides in facility upgrades and exhibits. Whenever General Salinas spoke about the Museum, her pride showed through. Her enthusiasm was contagious. She is the 6th woman to attain the rank of General in the Marine Corps and served her final years as a 2 star for Manpower Management at Marine Headquarters in Washington DC.

Two members the Museum's board of directors - Bill Paxton and Greg Spooner – deserve special note; Bill because of his unflagging devotion to all things Marine and Greg because of his authorship of books describing the rigor of boot camp and the importance of the Drill Instructor. The books that Greg wrote include "The Yellow Footprints To Hell and Back" and a biography of Marine legend, Sergeant Major Bill Paxton – "OOORAH!" Greg and Bill are both former Drill Instructors. I keep in touch with these inspirational fellow Marines by attending the quarterly breakfast meetings at MCRD..

Loss of Family Members

The early years of the new century brought a concentration of tragedy that brought me to my knees. I lost my wife of thirty years and mother of my four children. I lost my only son Mark and I lost my youngest daughter Robin. And, in all likelihood, I lost my oldest daughter, Ginny during this same time period.

Loss of Best Friends

I also lost my best friends. Frank Nakamura was the first to go. His passing was due to respiratory complications resulting from pneumonia. I visited Frank many times during his final days at Kaiser Hospital. There were times when I felt Frank would make it. He was always so upbeat. He never complained. He suffered some memory slippage but he remembered me and the things we had done together. To the very end, that same indomitable spirit that carried him through his WWII internment camp experience for Japanese Americans and his selection as a first Japanese American to make the first team on the University of Michigan's football team shone through. Frank was one of those few individuals you could trust implicitly and genuinely like. The girls liked Frank too, especially the waitresses at Perry's in El Cajon and the Panda Inn and Jimmy's in Santee.

I met Frank's two sons in his final days. One was the pastor of a Japanese-American Christian church in San Diego. The other son was a flight mechanic at Brown Field in south San Diego near the Mexican border. Frank was also very close to his unofficially adopted daughter, Lisa. Frank had taken her under his wing when she was a young girl. She watched over Frank in his last years even taking him into her home. Frank was in his early eighties when he passed.

Next we lost Bob Mendoza. Another great loss. I don't know the exact cause of Bob's death. It may have been his heart. I attended his funeral mass and the farewell military ceremony of an Army honor guard. I miss Bob's laughter, his great stories, his conscientiousness and the great tomales his wife, Lupe, would make around Christmas. But, above all, I miss a friend who was there to help when I needed it most. Bob came out of retirement to ensure our fiscal affairs were tip-top shape after the hectic days of our opening

Then we lost Costas, owner of Perry's restaurant and management companion, to cancer. What a loss. I don't think Costas missed a day of work since opening his restaurants. He worked seven days a week alternating between his El Cajon location and the one near Old Town. About five years before his passing, he sold his El Cajon restaurant to one of his employees. It continues to operate under the same name and with the same menu. Both restaurants have a large core of dedicated customers. His daughter Perry and wife Margaret have taken over the Old Town restaurant since his passing and maintain the same friendly and efficient atmosphere. Like many others, I miss Costas' personal and friendly greeting every time I entered his restaurants.. I know Costas understood the value of the owner's personal touch in running a business. He knew his customers and, over time, got to know their interests. When those interests coincided with his own passion for effective management practices, he cultivated a friendship. He was a modern day Plato. He enjoyed the role of mentor as well as business owner. I remember his buying a whole case of the books about customer relations and putting a copy in the hands of all his favorite patrons. The book was called "Crowning the Customer" by Feargal Quinn.

Costas was committed to sound management. Here, he followed the principles espoused by E. Edwards Deming. This was obvious to anyone who took note of the Deming photo that hung on the wall of his Old Town restaurant. Costas introduced me to the writings of British business philosopher Charles Handy and I made him a fan of Peter Drucker. Between the two of us, we had a very formidable library of works by the most influential business authors of the day. I really miss Costas and his mental stimulation

Then Harry Vorrath passed on, another cancer victim. I didn't know about Harry's passing until I dropped by his home to see how things were going. We had lost touch after our school closing. When his wife told me Harry died, you could have knocked me over with a feather. I knew Harry recently had a stent implanted to improve his blood circulation but I knew nothing about his prostate cancer. The last time I saw Harry he was still consulting in the Midwest and implementing his Positive Peer Culture. The last time I saw him he seemed healthy, upbeat and happy to be working again.

In our last conversation, I remember Harry telling me he felt he had several years of work left in him before he really retired. Harry and I were the same age and both had comparable religious life and Marine Corps experience in our younger years. Our approach to working with students also had similarities although Harry worked in the field of alternative education and I focused on the mainstream. Harry targeted problem students whose behavior was so bad they were committed to locked down facilities. His program was designed to change a selfish, non-conforming and disruptive young person to one who was considerate and attentive to the learning and personal needs of others. Harry's students learned that their success and best interests were served when they helped others.

Harry's approach eventually resulted in the removal of bars, unlocking of doors and mainstreaming of students. Although my teaching world is usually absent the challenges Harry undertook, I sometimes describe Harry's approach to my own students when I encounter some discipline problems. I remind students that I am a teacher not a policeman and that I expect them to police themselves. Then I write on the board something like this – "Please be Quiet. We're here to Learn". When a disruption occurs, I might have the whole class repeat these words in unison while looking in the direction of the offender. This is so unexpected by the offender that it often has the desired effect. I've used it but rarely. Thanks, Harry. I'll promote your legacy as long as I can.

Marsha's Family Loss

Marsha was still battling fibromyalgia when she got word that her mother had passed away. The funeral took place in Redding, a northern California town near Mt. Shasta. Marsha joined with her brother and sister for the service. All were born and raised in Redding where her father had also passed away a few years earlier. Her father had a very successful career in real estate and construction. With her mother's passing, there was a sizeable inheritance. When combined with Social Security and Medicare, Marsha had the cushion she needed for her own retirement. She was very generous with her financial gain buying her adopted daughter Lisa a new SUV. As for her son, Sean, also an adopted child, his natural mother appeared after Sean had graduated from high school. She was now in a position to give Sean a good home and finance his college education. Marsha felt that the opportunity offered Sean was better than what she could offer. All parties agreed. Sean went to Salt Lake City, became a Mormon, completed college, married, joined the marketing division of a major food supplier, bought a home in Arkansas and became the proud father of four sons. Marsha missed Sean but believed his natural parents were in a better position than she to support Sean's future success. It was my observation, however, that Marsha still occupied the number one spot in Sean's heart.

West Coast Swing

Marsha and I danced a lot. The two-step, line dances and East Coast swing topped our dance card with an occasional waltz and cha cha thrown in. We were regulars at In-Cahoots in Mission Valley or Mulvaney's (later the Wagon Wheel) in Santee. Our dance outings helped us maintain a semblance of normalcy during a period in which we both suffered the loss of individuals who were so close..

Travel was another welcome diversion. Marsha liked to travel and so did I. During this period we visited England, France, Belgium, Holland, Portugal, Spain, Morocco, Hawaii and Cancun. Marsha also liked pets so we had a spoiled cat and a pampered dog. Andy, the cat, was a beautiful, blue eyed Ragdoll and Amos, the dog, was a white, curly-haired cockapoo.

About this time, Marsha and I began taking West Coast Swing lessons. This dance was overtaking East Coast swing in popularity even on the country circuit. I saw it as a new challenge and fixed my sights on learning it. West Coast is danced to contemporary music and there is no ending to its moves and nuances. It goes well with Michael Jackson's Thriller and some of the beats popularized by Black Eyed Peas and Pit Bull. Dance movements are smooth and phrased to the music. Once caught up in West Coast there is no end to the creative moves the music can inspire. Most serious West Coast devotees are junkies when it comes to taking classes from those whose style of dancing set the standard and leads the pack. West Coast is subtle, smooth and sexy.

Our first lesson in West Coast swing was with Robert and Vicki Palladino. It took place in a small classroom on a Grossmont Adult Education campus. These were fun classes well suited for the beginner. Occasional disagreements between Vicki and Robert over the execution of a particular steps provided unexpected entertainment during the class.

Following the Adult Ed swing class, I joined a class being taught by Brick Robbins at the Mission Valley Inn. The dance floor at this hotel was small but a step up from the Grossmont facilities. But Brick soon changed his venue to the Cheek-to-Cheek dance studio in Pacific Beach, another step up. A stickler for basics and repetitive drills on footwork and hand holds, Brick, a student of a West Coast Swing icon, Skippy Blair, fueled my desire to be a better dancer. I was hooked on the dance but had a long way to go. The dance is dynamic and the patterns seem limitless. New moves are constantly emerging.

Marsha's fibromyalgia was limiting her movements and the turns and spins of West Coast swing movements didn't make matters any better. So early on, my appearance at swing lessons and dances became as solitary as trips to the gym. But partner rotations during classes and the usual availability of partners during regular dances minimized the inconvenience of not having a regular partner.

After Brick, I came under the tutelage of Mary Manzella, a dance champion who had a dance studio in her home where her many dancing trophies were on display.. But she used the dance facilities of Cheek-to-Cheek in Pacific Beach as her primary training and dance venue as well as the La Mesa's Women's club used by the San Diego Swing Club. Mary is a beautiful dancer and excellent instructor. She puts a lot of emphasis on styling and musicality. She is included in the California State's Dancing Hall of Fame. Mary has been on the dance scene for years, a tribute to her health and physique, An attractive blond, Mary moves like a twenty-something. She is also a frequent leader of shipboard dancing cruises.

After a year or two with Mary, I gravitated to the master - Michael Kiehm. Michael is a champion, a master teacher and probably the nation's foremost exponent of West Coast swing. His Starlight Ballroom is home to the highest concentration of award-winning instructors and dancers in the country. Those of us who live in San Diego consider ourselves lucky to have him. Michael is our inspiration and model. We consider him a national treasure.

Michael produces an internationally acclaimed 3 day workshop each year in San Diego. It is called Swing Diego and takes place in May at the Town and Country Hotel in San Diego's Mission Valley. The event attracts dancers from around the country and around the world. His Starlight dance studio is a bee hive of activity for dancers pursuing proficiency in dances ranging from West Coast to ballroom and tango to hip hop.

Marsha and Robin

Meanwhile, off the dance floor, relations between Marsha and me were going south. We were bickering over too many inconsequential things. I now view bickering as the prelude to a break-up. It was that way with Bernie, that way with Maria and now it was being repeated with Marsha. She told me on a couple of occasions she wanted her house back – meaning she wanted me out. I would soon oblige. It seems my personal relations with women have about a seven year shelf life.

About this time, Robin dropped in on us after her break-up with a San Francisco boyfriend and a brief stay with Charlotte in La Canada. As is so often happens in divorce, their Pacifica home went up for sale and a court-ruling split custody and visitation rights for their only child Amber. Charlotte had some strong negative feelings about Robin, her former husband Steve and her choice of boy- friends. As for me, I was just glad to see Robin after such a long period of no communication, going back as far as her marriage to Steve. My hope was that we could recapture a relationship that existed before the wedding fallout. She was the youngest and the smallest. She always wished she were taller. But she was funny, good natured, a talented dancer, and a marathon runner. She also liked to sail.

Robin was looking for a job, had some interviews and finally settled in on a job after a couple misfires. She had a good paying job as an office manager in San Francisco and found her skills in demand in San Diego. When she was working and living with us in Santee, she was a night owl. She met someone who shared her boating interests, had a boat and was a member of the San Diego Yacht Club. Robin took up with him and they rented a place in Point Loma. For awhile, things seemed to be going fairly well for Robin though not well enough for Amber to join her. Charlotte had a better overview of the situation than I and had a negative view of Robin's lifestyle. But I had been out of the picture with Robin for so long I was cheered by her presence. I felt I recovered a long lost daughter.

Mark

Then the world began to crumble beneath me. I got a call on the morning of Father's Day, June 18, 2006 from County Coroner.

"Is this Mr. Byron?"

"Yes."

"Do you have a son Mark?"

"Yes."

"I'm afraid we have some very bad news. Your son Mark died earlier this morning."

I was stunned. I couldn't believe it. I had seen Mark just a few days earlier. He looked healthy to me.

"What!!! I can't believe it. What happened."

"We received a call from one of the residents where Mark was living telling us that when Mark did not respond to a wake-up call that morning, they entered his room and found him dead. Our autopsy report will be ready in a few days."

Just like that. I still couldn't believe it. The loss was yet to sink in. There were things I had to do – tell Charlotte, Robin, relatives and friends, make funeral arrangements, arrange for a commemorative service and gather up his belongings. I arranged for Mark to be cremated and made arrangements for relatives and friends to join Charlotte, Robin and myself for a commemoration at the Mission Bay Hilton hotel. I later got word from the Coroner that Mark's death was heart-related.

I set a date for committing Mark's ashes to the Pacific and arranged for a Marine honor guard from a local Marine detachment to give Mark a final salute. Charlotte, her husband and my grandkids, cousins Jack and Bob O'Donnell and Christa boarded a dive boat in Quivira Basin and set out to sea. I scattered Mark's ashes about two miles from shore. I couldn't think of anything more fitting than for Mark who spent so much of his time underwater in the Pacific have his ashes joined with those of his mother. It brought back the memory of Mark's mother's ashes being likewise sprinkled into the Pacific some six years earlier. Charlotte made all the arrangements then. Now I was the one busy making arrangements for Mark. I was so busy making arrangements that the shock and sorrow of his death didn't hit home until a few weeks later. He was only fifty.

Death is not supposed to come in that order.. Bernie, presumably Ginny and now Mark. I remembered Mark as a toddler and built like a little tank. He loved the water and liked hammering things. Then he grew into a long drink of water whose interests encompassed every macho thing you could think of from scuba-diving to parachute jumping. All this despite his epilepsy. He also did construction work where his childhood love of hammering continued. But the best paying and steadiest job he ever had was aboard an oil spill recovery ship, several of which were built by the oil companies after the Exxon Valdez oil spill. Mark was part of the crew whose ship covered the west coast. When in port, Mark was part of a teaching team that instructed fishing boat operators on the procedures to be used in rounding-up of oil in the event of a spill. But Mark got caught in an employee cutback and went back to construction.

Mark didn't have an easy life. His epilepsy was a challenge. But given these tough circumstances, I admired his guts. His heroes were Lloyd Bridges of Sea Hunt, Clint Eastwood and Steve McQueen. Although his circle of friends was small, the sea provided a companionship and safe haven in life and a final resting place in death.

Soon after Mark's death I told Marsha I would be out of her condo by the end of the month. I was. Finding a place, however, was taking more time than I thought. Robin put me up at her place for a couple weeks. During this time I found a place that worked out well – the De Anza Resort on Mission Bay.

Christa

Christa Govan, the charismatic and charming owner of two, not-so-mobile homes in the De Anza park, rented out part of her home to me. These mobile homes at De Anza Cove were manufactured shortly after WWII but were located in one of the choicest areas in San Diego. The park was on an area of the back bay just across from Fiesta Island. Most of the homes have as much if not more square footage as a standard home. They come in 1-2-3 bedroom models, usually with two parking spaces and enough room for a couple of outside storage sheds, a porch and patio. But the real value lies in the location and view.

De Anza, now called Mission Bay Park, is one of the most desirable living spots on the coast. Major improvements to the Mission Bay aquatic area were made some years ago by the Army Corps of Engineers. These improvements attracted several major hotels. The city of San Diego is the designated agent of the property. Eventually, the land will revert to public use either in the form of additional public park land or a combination of public-commercial usage. Litigation to compensate the residents for loss of their homes as well as relocation expenses has been ongoing for several years. When the court case is finally settled, it is anticipated that a fair compensation will be reached and that residents will find their way to comparable living quarters. Christa has been a leader in keeping the residents informed as to the progress of legal proceedings. She estimates that De Anza will remain open anywhere from 3 to 8 years during which time she is planning to develop a new manufactured home site comparable to De Anza.

Robin in her Point Loma kitchen. Final days. 2008

Christa Govan, granddaughter Amber, the author and Amber's step-mother at Amber's high school graduation in Pacifica 2009

Mark in his final days. 2006

Meanwhile, the park's Homeowners Association has a top legal team on contract to pursue fair treatment and just compensation. So far, that team has won some significant awards from the city in punitive damages for the harassment the residents suffered at the hands of a city-hired security company and their intimidating actions designed to force residents to move. Action by the park's attorneys has delayed the park's closure and, as of this writing, proceedings are in motion to determine a fair compensation for the properties and relocation costs. Christa has been at the center of this controversy almost from the beginning. She was publisher of a park newsletter for some time and has been active in all park proceedings. She also maintains oversight of several park properties on behalf of absent owners. Given Christa's background as a Montessori School director, small business owner, world traveler, real estate agent and member of a family in the film and jewelry business, it is not surprising that Christa is in the forefront of park doings and putting in motion plans for a new park to accommodate residents when De Anza finally closes.

Hip Replacement

Soon after moving in with Christa, a hip that had been bothering me for couple years had to be replaced. This knocked me off the dance scene for about a year. If you do a lot of dancing, sooner or later the wear and tear on the joints can take their toll. The cartilage cushioning the swivel of the femor in the hip socket just wears out. Motion then becomes painful and cortisone relief is only temporary. Right now, the permanent solution involves replacing the worn bone area with a metal socket and shank. I am sure this procedure will be replaced with a less invasive method in the future. Perhaps an injection of a cartilage-like substance into the joint area could replace the major surgery now involved.

With a metal hip, you can expect to set off metal detectors at airport inspection points or state or federal building entrances. Depending on the individual, recovery can take anywhere from a several months to a year. In my case, it took about a year – an unbearably long time for a dancer. You graduate from a walker to a cane and finally to your own two feet. Depending on the extensiveness of the bone that is ground to make a smooth seating for the metal socket, you may need a lift in your shoe to even up your leg length. When I returned to the dancing scene a year later, it took an additional two years to regain most of my former dexterity and flexibility. Christa was a selfless supporter during my recovery. It was also a time when I saw more of Robin than I had since we lived in Anaheim Hills.

Courses Continue

During this time I developed and presented two unique courses for the Osher and Oasis foundations. One course included a review of the charters defining the governance structure of the original colonies before the American Revolution. The colonial governance structures under the crown were examined and compared to the follow-on structures of the new States. The classroom and computer accommodations were ideal especially at San Diego State. Internet access to the Yale University digitized document repository made image projections easy. This environment stimulated discussion.

Another course featured a comparative analysis of political party platforms. At each presidential election, parties summarize their stand on key issues and publicize them in a party document called a platform. A party's position on issues like slavery and nullification is an indication of how the nation might move given the election of certain candidates. You can see a civil war looming, an expansionist movement growing, immigration becoming an issue, and railroad expansion enjoying the support of the leading parties. A platform approach to identifying issues is as comprehensive and realistic as it gets. Platforms, key historical documents and good presidential biographies make for an exciting survey of America's past.

The appeal of my World Affairs course lay in its real time dynamics and scope. How well a class can interact in discussions on major contemporary issues is a reflection of the scope and depth of their knowledge. The perennial popularity of classes in the World Affairs genre is also a reflection of the maturity of individuals willing to present their opinions before others who might disagree. It is the height of democracy, an American town hall in action It counterbalances the often doctrinaire interpretations of events by some talking heads on radio and TV.

Some opinion shapers with access to TV and radio have enjoyed minimal competition from opposing viewpoints. But the digital world of tweets, email, blogs and internet are providing competition in the sheer volume of information access. Who knows what the outcome of a Ross Perot presidential bid might have been had the nation been as digitally wired as now? Look at the influence of a Tea Party. Look at the unpredictable demonstrations led by the Occupiers. Look at the millions demanding jobs and a better life, toppling leaders who were expected to hold power indefinitely, people not afraid to die. No matter how these revolts play out, the current rash of uprisings in parts of the world where people are throwing their own lives on the line for jobs, a better life and a real voice in their own governance should tell us something – like too few have too much.

While it's almost a hundred and fifty years since our Civil war and two hundred and thirty some since our own revolution, the democracy we practice in our republic is still evolving. We expect our government to safeguard our liberties, provide a common defense and promote our well-being but in recent years we've witnessed the emergence of a contentious streak far beyond the typical contrast of political party philosophies. That contentious streak has impaired our ability to focus on jobs, infrastructure renewal, immigration reform, housing, education, health care and protecting the environment. Is getting our fiscal house in order really the number one priority or is it the tail wagging the dog? The answer most would expect is "both" It can be done.

What does a widening gap between the rich and the poor and a battered middle class tell us? That opposing political forces within the nation are paralyzing action? Were we to turn up the heat on infrastructure renewal and a return to the draft of America's youth, we would have to invite our retirees back into the workforce. And, with proper wage scales, we could establish a decent standard of living for all.

As for our governance, the battle between strict and loose constructionists continues. Yet, in our two hundred thirty some years of existence, we've added but 27 amendments to our Constitution, the first ten of which, our Bill of Rights, were added 2 years after the Constitution's ratification. Two amendments involved Prohibition, one cancelling the other. How can our Constitution be considered immutable if the document itself contains provisions for amending – although not an easy process. Maybe our whole governance system needs reviewing. Jefferson, in fact, was an advocate of future Constitutional Conventions so subsequent generations could ensure a Constitution suited to the needs of the day.

While several provisions of our Constitution are likely to change over time – the electoral college, terms of office, life time Supreme Court appointments, congressional boundaries and a vice-presidential link to the Senate, we are culturally slow to change anything absent a cataclysmic event. Witness the length of time before a nullification doctrine erupted in Civil war or the time it took for women to get the vote. For some, changing the Constitution is tantamount to changing the Bible.

Changes that I expect over time include discontinuance of the electoral college system, removal of life terms for Supreme Court justices, term limits on Congress, extraction of the Vice President from presiding over the Senate or a merger of the upper and lower houses into a single body – like Nebraska. Benjamin Franklin saw merit in a single house. He saw the upper and lower division as a class divide similar to the British House of Commons and House of Lords. As regards to equal votes for each State in the Senate, States with more livestock than people have the same voting power as Senators from States with huge populations like California, New York, Texas or Illinois. Although the basis for equal State representation in the Senate was a compromise necessary to get a majority of the original colonies to sign on to the Constitution, the danger of a minority population thwarting the will of the majority, at least in the Senate, still exists.

It seems that the world is experiencing upheavals in parts of the world under dictatorial control for decades. These are spontaneous eruptions. People from countries like Tunisia, Egypt, Bahrain, Yemen, Jordan, Libya, Syria and Turkey are predominantly young and are demanding jobs and a better life. They are tired of the disconnect between those in power and governments unable to improve their lot.

Two early forecasters of the disconnect between society and its government were Alvin and Heidi Toffler. They popularized the onset of the information age with their best-selling book, "The Third Wave". Later, the disconnects were further publicized in their 1970 best-seller "Future Shock" and again in their 1994 book "Creating a New Civilization". These books are prophetic. They have withstood the test of time and should be required reading in schools, government and corporations.

In the US, disconnects are seen in a two party system whose philosophic divide creates gridlock and continuous debate. Splinter groups hold major parties captive. An election schedule holds people hostage to a calendar. The. government cannot seem to fire up the will or energy to make major infrastructure tasks proceed with dispatch – things like high speed transport, new cities, new power grids, new water and sewer systems, new bridges and alternative energy sources.

Hideaway

I do a lot of my reading at an ideal hideaway. It is a small cafe at Quivira Basin in Mission Bay. Here I enjoy uninterrupted reading at a small table by a window overlooking a yacht basis. Pelicans circle overhead then land on the water as fishing boats return and throw some of their catch overboard. Harbor seals glide under and over the water competing with birds for fishing boat remnants. A nearby dive boat is the one we used to commit Mark and Robin's ashes to the deep.

Patriotism Resurgence

On September 11, 2001, events occurred that refocused national priorities on the threat at hand. In New York, the twin towers were struck. In Washington DC the Pentagon was struck.. In Pennsylvania, a plane intended to strike our capitol was down in Shanksville. thanks to the brave initiative of passengers and crew. More lives were lost than at Pearl Harbor. Suddenly, the nation was mobilized and a national response was set in motion. We were united in a just cause – the search and destruction of Bin Laden and his Al Queda terrorist organization.

We have been in battle now for over ten years. Our campaign in Iraq has concluded. Our troops have been withdrawn. The battle in Afghanistan is winding down as Afghan forces are preparing to assume responsibility for their own national security. The President has announced our withdrawal from Afghanistan in 2014. 9/11 that brought us together like Pearl Harbor is the longest military campaign in our nation's history. We are fighting an un-uniformed enemy with no territorial boundaries.

An excellent read on Afghan history is Stephen Tanner's 2009 edition of "Afghanistan, A Military History from Alexander the Great to the War

Against the Taliban". A reading of this book will temper any visions of national pacification.

A graceful extraction while continuing to protect American interests and promote our values is not easy. We are a major player in a region characterized by competing religious sects, tribal alignments, linguistic differences, forbidding terrain, weapons of mass destruction and little experience with the governance necessary to cure the economic malaise. The massive and spontaneous uprisings in motion in so many different parts of the world beg for an economic and political resolutions on a global scale.

Ultimately, the best hope for improving life for all lies in education. As regards education in Afghanistan, especially for women, there has been no better advocate than Greg Mortenson. Greg, an American mountain climber who sustained injuries while climbing the Hindu Kush and Karakorum mountain range was treated and restored to health by Afghan villagers. By way of thanks, he promised to return and build something they wanted dearly – a school, especially one for girls. He delivered on his promise by building not just one school but several.

In his two best selling books, one published in 2006 and titled "Three Cups of Tea" and another published in 2009 and titled "Stones into Schools", Greg makes a strong case for building schools in the tribal areas throughout Afghanistan. The books and donations have generated the financial wherewithal to build schools in Taliban-threatened environments. Mortensen's books have been made part of cultural orientations given to many troops headed for Afghanistan.

There are some other 'must' reads for anyone seeking more in-depth knowledge of the war and related developments instigated by the 9/11 attack. These include "Fiasco" by Thomas Ricks and "Cobra II" by Michael Gordon and General Bernard Trainor. In a 2004 book called "Battle Ready", Tom Clancy collaborates with Marine General Tony Zinni to provide a unique insider view and blunt assessment of events leading-up to the Iraq invasion.

Other notable reads include the 2006 "Iraq Study Group Report" co-chaired by Lee Hamilton and James Baker III and the 2007 US Army/ Marine Corps Counterinsurgency Field Manual with forwards by Army General David Petraeus and Marine General James Amos. Another 2007 book called "Blackwater" by Jeremy Scahill gives an account of Blackwater, a private security organization which has since changed its name to Xee. This account publicized the little known role of private security organizations and, to some extent, the costs of these operations from CIA and State Department coffers.

These best-selling books, newspapers and periodicals have also highlighted fiscal mismanagement and contractor fraud triggering investigations and tighter oversight. But we had our own share political and fiscal debacles just prior to the invasion including the Bush-Gore election, the Enron and Tyco scandals, and the modus operandi of our major oil company cartels Books that contributed significantly to our awareness of these issues included the 2002 book "The Best Democracy Money Can Buy" by Greg Palast, the 2003 book "Pigs at the Trough" by Arianna Huffington, the 2004 book "Confessions of an Economic Hit Man by John Perkins and the 2005 book "The World Is Flat" by Thomas Friedman.

CSPAN has been a premier source of information with its coverage of congressional hearings, book reviews and televising public interest meetings. But even though we enjoy an information overload, it still feels as though too much time is devoted to the trivial and that coverage of substantive issues is too often slanted.

Robin's Battle

For a while it looked as though Robin's life was making a turnaround. She was working and had a boyfriend who owned a sail boat and had a yacht club membership. Robin was heavily involved with the boating community. She frequently helped with the many boat races and genuinely seemed to be enjoying herself. But then she began having difficulty swallowing and noticed blood in her cough. Robin's checked into the hospital for some tests and the results were not what we wanted to hear. Robin had esophageal cancer. She was shaken but determined to overcome it. We were there to support her all the way.

Then Robin began a feeding regimen that wasn't easy. It meant feeding tubes and a strict limit on what she could take orally. Dietary habits changed dramatically. The only things she could get down her throat easily were things like yogurt, pudding, soup, ice cream and liquids. To provide the nutrition she needed, a feeding tube was inserted directly into her stomach. Then came chemo and hair loss. Robin was weakened. She tired easily but she kept up a walking routine. Her treatments seemed to be working. Her oral food intake began to increase. Her blond hair grew back. Lance Armstrong, a prostate cancer survivor and the winner of seven Tour de France bicycle races became Robin's new hero. It was such a sad letdown for so many when Lance was stripped of his Tour de France victories because of performance enhancing procedures.

Then came the great news that her cancer appeared to be in remission. We were elated. She resumed her boating interests with Steve and she began making plans to go back to work or school. But then came a relapse. She was re-hospitalized and went back into chemo treatments. We spent as much time as possible at the hospital keeping her supplied with her favorite Starbuck's coffee and MacDonald milkshakes. She seemed to be improving. But little after midnight on Christmas day Steve called me with shocking news.

"Bob, I've got bad news. Robin died tonight around midnight."

"What! I can't believe it. We just saw her a few hours ago. She looked better than ever.

What happened?"

"All I know is that around midnight, Robin had trouble breathing and they were unable to revive her."

I was stunned. I couldn't believe it. Christa and I had been with Robin just hours earlier. She looked good to me and very relaxed. I was grief stricken. As in Mark's case, the activity of making final arrangements helped submerge my sorrow. I made the same arrangements for Robin that I made for Mark just a year and a half earlier. We were joined by family and relatives on a dive boat out of Quivira Basin. We motored out to sea once again, this time scattering Robin's ashes. Afterwards, family and friends gathered at Christa's De Anza home to commemorate Robin's passing and to celebrate the happier memories of her brief life.

It's not supposed to be this way. In the natural order of things, children bury their parents. Ginny was presumed gone, probably at the beginning of the decade – something I have no closure on. Mark passed on suddenly on Father's Day 2006. Robin passes on Christmas day, 2008. Their mother and my former wife Bernie passed on in 2001. What a decade of loss and tragedy. We have dwindled to a precious few – only my daughter Charlotte remains and her three daughters – Aryn, Noor and Hanna - and Robin's daughter, Amber.

The decade was witness not only to the loss of family members but my best friends as well – Frank Nakamura, Bob Mendoza, Costas Georgakopoulos and Harry Vorrath. My triple by-pass no doubt prolonged my own journey on this planet. I still have work to do.

Triple By-Pass

A couple months after Robin's passing, I began experiencing a shortness of breath on the dance floor. Following a night visit to Sea World where Christa and I rode the observation tower for a glance at the city's night lights, I told Christa I was going to check into the emergency room just to see what was going on. I told her I wanted to go alone and would probably be back in a couple hours. After some tests, those expected couple of hours translated into a prolonged stay in the Emergency room and eventual admission to the hospital. That I was even admitted to the hospital is a tribute to the urgings of my daughter Charlotte, my doctor son-in-law Ayad and Christa. After all the diagnostics, I thought a stent would be all that was needed. But the physician thought differently. By-pass surgery would be required. It turned out to be a triple by-pass. Had I not undergone that operation, I was assured that my next heart-related problem would have been my last. But I recovered from my heart surgery faster than the hip. I was back teaching within a month.

Middle Schools and High Schools Revisited

Working as a visiting teacher for San Diego Unified and Sweetwater Union High reconnected me with youth. Although I remained engaged with college level classes for adults, I enjoyed being close to young people and their contagious enthusiasm. The young students were as yet unspoiled by the complications of adult life. It reminded me of earlier days as director of a training program for displaced engineers. I began that program on a high school campus in Orange County. The youthful vitality of the high school environment was a real morale booster for the participating former aerospace professionals who had lost their jobs and were preparing for work in the public sector.

I am very conscious of the trust I enjoy as a secondary level teacher with the power to influence young minds. Having the opportunity to teach and guide students in many different schools has given me a unique look at student performance and classroom conditions throughout two major school districts in San Diego county.

Each campus usually mirrors the socio-economics and racial diversity of the surrounding neighborhood. San Diego has a very diverse population. Although a school's location will determine the dominant racial mix, you can find Asian, Hispanic, Black and White on practically every campus. On campuses close to the Mexican border, Spanish is the dominant language between classes. Spanish is also dominant even in the administrative areas where employees are dealing with many Spanish speaking parents. With so many students coming from homes where Spanish is spoken, the kids are comfortable with either language and speak unaccented English, an employment plus in this part of the country.

My classroom assignments usually involve carrying out the regular teacher's lesson plan. It is interesting to note the similarity of academic progression for similar subjects in different schools. Material is covered almost in lockstep with a goal of successful test performance and graduation. But lockstep schedules and large class sizes can work at cross-purposes when it comes to developing critical thinking skills. Class size while not a problem in large, lecture style classes at the college level is a problem at the middle and high school level where motivation and attention spans are still in developmental stages. At the pre-college level, young minds are in a formative stage and individual guidance is very helpful. Then too there is the element of the physical growth and a need for exercise breaks. Block schedules – double the length of the usual 55 minute class – are usually too long for most students to stay on task especially if there is little or no time for physical movement.

A frequent time waster for a visiting teacher is having students watch a video prescribed by the regular teacher. Having grown up with a steady diet of videos and TV at home, this passive activity bores most students.. However, research on the Internet is an entirely different process. This requires the active engagement of the student. I take advantage of using this tool whenever possible. Another time waster is having all students take turns in reading aloud. So few students are good at this that it is painful to complete the exercise. It becomes just too obvious who is able to read and get the idea as opposed to those who struggle to read one word at a time. Vocal reading skills should be developed as part of a separate Public Speaking or Oral Reading class.

I usually make it a practice to engage middle and high school students in an activity that combines listening, note taking, Internet research, essay writing and knowledge sharing. For example, I will review the process of note-taking itself and then explain how to use notes as an outline for an Internet search and an essay. I emphasize the importance of good listening then proceed to lecture briefly on a topic relevant to their course. At the conclusion, I invite questions the way members of the press act at White House briefings. Then I release them to Internet research for additional material for their essay. I remind them to budget their time so their research and essay can be completed by the end of the class. When time is available, I have them share what they have learned independently. A few students may be called on to read their essays aloud.

The interaction with the Internet is an enjoyable experience for most students. They are at home with things digital. Our kids have grown up on text messaging, Itunes, interactive computer games, the Internet and cell phones. Developing the habit of self-teaching by routinely searching the Internet to answer questions or expand one's knowledge puts the student on the glide path to continuous and independent learning. Although there is still a shortfall of Internet availability in some classrooms, the gap is being closed rapidly.

I enjoy being on the cusp of the school of tomorrow. The school of the future is evolving before our eyes. The Internet, Kindle-like reading devices, digital camera projectors and software libraries covering the spectrum of academics are here now and in use. Kindle-like devices are not only cost-effective but save a lot of wear and tear on kids' backs. Oversized textbooks are too big and heavy for kids to lug around. Digital texts are easier to revise and cheaper than print.

With knowledge at one's fingertips, students can learn at a pace suited to their learning abilities. Students should be encouraged to move through study materials at a rate consistent with their comprehension. At the same time, a student should be encouraged to self-teach. Students can progress at their own rate and that rate can be monitored by teachers. Many computer programs provide immediate performance feedback.to the student. When student weaknesses are detected, remedial software is available to help overcome deficiencies.

Without the stimulus of interaction, whether electronic or a teacher's use of Socratic methods, a sizeable portion of students would have difficulty staying on task. There was a time when I was a firm supporter of block schedules – class times double the length of the standard 55 minutes. But confining young students to small classrooms for two hours is too long. Standard 55 minutes classes are just about right with more time between classes for bathroom breaks, a drink of water and leg stretching. Except for lab classes, computer classes and programs that physically engage the student, like drama, music or sports, maintaining the attention of 30-40 students over a two hour block is practically an unnatural act. My hat is off to anyone who can keep average students at the middle or high school level productively engaged in a typical classroom for more than an hour without digital interaction.

As regards classroom discipline, it is important to remember that each class is different. The experienced teacher recognizes this and tailors classroom discipline accordingly. The visiting teacher seldom has the same rapport with students as the regular teacher. Nevertheless, distractions can be minimized. Disciplinary action is also an art. On occasion I have found Harry Vorrath's approach useful. Harry would groom student leaders to inspire others and lead in the putdown of class disruptions. When I sensed the likelihood of a rowdy class, I would tell them the Harry Vorrath story then write on the board "Please Be Quiet. We're Here to Learn". When a distraction arose that I wanted to squelch, I would ask the class to repeat out loud and in unison the message printed on the board. This usually has the desired effect but this must be used sparingly otherwise the novelty wears off. The real trick to good classroom management is to be able to communicate clearly to the students at the very beginning of the class what the goals are for the period. Once goals are set and clearly understood by all the students, the combination lecture, Internet research, essay and report is a consistent winner.

There are many "improvement needed" conditions in our public schools. One is the classroom itself. Most are too cluttered. How a regular teacher navigates in a classroom plastered with rules, exhortations, a jumble of historical photos and a desktop buried in test papers is beyond me. Disarray seems to be the rule in too many classrooms. Ideally, the classroom should be stripped for action – like an operating room. The basic equipment should include a smart board, digital projector, Internet workstations, white boards, comfortable seating and adequate desk space. All unrelated items should be excluded from the classroom, including backpacks, skateboards, musical instruments, etc. However, since locker space is not always available, the burden of toting backpacks from class to class still exists. But relief may be on the way. A lot of new school construction is taking place throughout San Diego. Hopefully, the issue of storage space for student belongings is being addressed. Perhaps the biggest unaddressed factor of all is teacher input in the design of classrooms and other educational facilities. The clutter found in too many classrooms today should be a clue that teachers simply do not have enough space to comfortably execute their mission. Teachers must be brought into the architectural design planning phase at the very beginning.

As for textbooks, there is much to be desired. Relief in digital form, however, is coming. Right now, the size and weight of some texts discourage their use. Kindle and iPad style devices should soon make the classic hard copy text obsolete. The digital advantage in terms of costs, ease of handling and ease of updating are obvious. With regards to hard copy texts, especially those dealing with history, they are such a patchwork of summaries, photos and quizzes that getting any sense of continuity or depth is difficult at best. Using good historical biographies of presidents and other notable figures would provide a much better and in-depth understanding of our nation's past, give the student a better sense of a historical timeline and provide a better appreciation of the individuals and documents that identify us as Americans.

As for the study of a foreign language, I believe we are starting to get it right. We are introducing our youngest students to a foreign language in their earliest years. There is such practical value in being bi-lingual especially in a border area like San Diego.

I also prefer that students wear a school uniform and name badge. Many charter schools have uniform requirements as do many traditional campuses. I would also like to see students take more personal responsibility for keeping the classroom and school grounds clean like picking up trash even if not their own. I also think that many schools start too early.

As regards school and class size, I find smaller is better. Charter schools typically have a smaller student population than traditional schools. Charter schools have on average a student population of about 600. Some are even smaller. But there are also instances where a traditional school converts to charter status bringing its entire student population along with it. Helix High School in La Mesa is a case in point. It converted to charter status and brought along its entire student population of over 2000. But smaller student bodies are characteristic of most charter schools. Charter operators find that smaller is better in terms of student-teacher relationships and academic performance. The influence of charter schools on traditional schools can be seen in the creation of mini-schools with different emphasis on several traditional campuses. This emulation of charter schools is consistent with the legislative intent of lawmakers when the charter school law was passed.

Another example of smaller-is-better is the AVID (Advancement Via Individual Determination) program. This program provides academic support to students who want to go to college but whose grades are not up to the mark. Once accepted into the program, students work in small groups under the tutelage of college students. I first became acquainted with this program while forming my own charter school. AVID and I were targeting the same category of students – students capable of much higher academic performance but needed to be motivated and placed in a better learning environment.

Were you to look into an AVID classroom, you would observe a class of about twenty students broken into clusters, each focused on a different subject: algebra, geometry, English, social studies. One or two college or graduate level students would be guiding the academic work of each cluster. Student motivation and desire to learn would be obvious. AVID has an enviable track record for college placement.

Harry Vorrath's Positive Peer Culture works with a comparably small student leader program. Even the US Marine Corps builds on a small group - a fire team of four Marines. Small size facilitates communication. Charters, AVID, Positive Peer Culture and the US Marine Corps all use small unit cohesion to advantage as the basic building block for their operating success.

Let's not forget the teachers. Teachers need greater recognition of their professional standing. One very tangible way of doing this is to provide individual office space and better facilities for teacher conferences and eating facilities. None of the districts I have worked for provide individual office space for teachers. But reasons for not doing so go back to early construction considerations. Most pre-college school buildings were never designed with individual office spaces for teachers at the pay grade level of pre-college teachers. But as classroom configurations change to accommodate the new digital teaching environment, a teacher's space requirements must be considered as well. They need more space for research, developing presentations, planning projects, counseling and material storage.

Resource Pool – Visiting Teachers

I've proposed using the pool of visiting teachers to staff any new mini-school on traditional campuses. The visiting teacher pool contains the spectrum of teaching capabilities ready made for staffing such schools. Smaller schools might even opt for charter status with its own governance and budget. If smaller schools did attain charter status and remained on the mainstream campus, their cost for facilities would be minimal. The concept of schools within a school goes a long way towards meeting the goal of a smaller school and smaller class sizes. The visiting teacher pool would make an ideal resource for staff. Given the right leadership, charter school formation could be in the wings.

West Coast Swing and Michael Kiehm

While teaching can consume the better part of a day, dancing can consume the better part of a night. Dancing classes usually take place at night in deference to the adult participants who, for the most part, hold day jobs. For me, classes reinforce good habits and keep me in a learning mode. For a free spirit like me, classes, no matter the time of day, help me maintain a semblance of orthodoxy that dance partners expect. But west coast swing encourages innovation which is why I like it. Once beyond the introductory level of basic steps and moves, you will be more concerned with matching your body movement to the music and stimulating complimentary moves from your partner. This is where the joy of the dance happens.

But in the start-up phase, you learn the basic 6 or 8 count, the slotted dance floor concept, a right and left side pass, an overhead turn, a tuck, a whip, a sugar push, a barrel roll and a hammer lock. With a mastery of these moves, you are ready to have some fun on the dance floor. It seems the only limit to the sequence and combination of moves is one's own imagination and physical dexterity.

Michael Kiehm is a master of movement and styling. The music he selects for his dance classes is also masterful. It makes repetitive drills as enjoyable as a night out on the typical dance scene. Unfortunately, I have the same weakness remembering the names of songs I like to dance to as I had with remembering the names of the folk dances or country tunes I liked so much. But he is able to create the mood and field the music that made a night or day under his tutelage a real joy. His Starlight Ballroom on El Cajon Boulevard not far from my San Diego State alma mater could accommodate well over a hundred dance partners. Michael is a dance icon. We were followers of the lean, silver haired master of the dance.

Michael's teaching style is one that the best dance teachers emulate. His instruction begins with having couples execute an easy, basic move. This establishes student confidence. Following a basic step, the first segment of a new pattern is demonstrated a few times. Students then replicate the move and repeat it until the instructor is satisfied the students can execute the move correctly. Then, before going on to the next segment, a partner change takes place. This gives everyone an opportunity to dance with different people. This also provided additional practice and a chance to work on weaknesses. Once this process is completed, the full pattern is executed to music. I've always preferred group lessons to private because of the multiple partner changes and conditioning for the actual dance environment.

Michael's personal example and his classes set a high standard. He moves so smoothly even the simplest moves looks intricate. His classes have made me conscious of my tendency to overcomplicate a move, of being too stiff when holding a partner or turning a partner in a way that could cause injury. The classes also help me execute patterns I find intricate. Rising to the challenge of Michael's classes has helped me improve my dancing significantly. His c lasses have been a gateway to continuing self-improvement.

A team of extraordinary dance instructors works out of Michael's Starlight studio. Members include nationally acclaimed champion dancers like Michael John Kielbasa (Michael's nephew), Parker Dearborn, Michael's sister Carmen,Tony DeBenedetta, Patty Vo, Brandi Tobias and Don

Kergil. This talented cluster of dance champions provides instruction in dances ranging from Salsa, Hustle and Tango to Night Club 2 Step, Fox Trot, Quick Step and Waltz.

I began attending Michael's classes just before a hip replacement knocked me off the scene for almost a year. When I resumed dancing, I was knocked off the scene again with a triple by-pass. The by-pass meant another several months of withdrawal. You don't appreciate the joy and exercise that dance provides until you are knocked off the playing field. But I'm back in action again.

If a good instructor is defined by the performance capability of his students and the size of his following, Michael is, hands down, the best. It is always stimulating to learn from a master. Michael is a recognized leader of West Coast swing at home and abroad. His smoothness and musicality are standouts. He gets around, knows what the young and in-crowd are doing, competes, judges, leads a stable of the best dance instructors in town at his Starlight ballroom, produces videos and hosts an annual 3 day West Coast event at the San Diego Town and Country Hotel and Convention Center that attracts participants from all over the world.

For the past few years, I have attended weekend workshops at hotels in San Diego and Palm Springs. Conventions are a dancer's delight especially if you are a competitor. So many dancers like to compete that time for social dancing is often compressed to the chagrin of those there for workshops and social dancing. Nevertheless, it can be said that competition sharpens dance execution and keeps performance levels high. Judges are sticklers for standards even within the innovative context of West Coast swing.

Weekend workshops usually attract hundreds from all over the country and abroad. Canada, France, the UK and Switzerland regularly have a strong presence. Michael, Dawn, Michael's nephew Michael John and Parker Dearborn have done much to extend West Coast swing's influence at home and abroad.

While Michael's SwingDiego attracts dancers from all over the world, similar events take place yearly in Palm Springs, Los Angeles, Anaheim, San Francisco. Phoenix and Tucson. Cruise liners have also gotten into the act and some local swing clubs have rented harbor cruise boats for a night of dining and dancing on the water.

There is an old Army ballad that General MacArthur popularized in his farewell address to Congress - "Old Soldiers Never Die, They Just Fade Away." If you substituted the word "dancers" for "soldiers" the words would ring just as true.

Dance Clubs

San Diego is a dancing town. Once you link up with any club, you will soon find your way to dance sites all over town. You could dance every night of the week.

West Coast swing has a devoted band of followers and there are clubs dedicated to that interest. Clubs catering to a particular dance style provide a venue and an affordable outlet. Many clubs are also more than one dimensional. Making it into the music mix of some clubs are the cha cha, salsa, hustle, waltz and two step. The top West Coast swing dance clubs in the San Diego area include the San Diego Swing Dance Club, Innovations, Patty Wells' studio, Tango del Rey in Pacific Beach and Michael Kiehm's Starlight Dance studio where Parker Dearborn leads his Project Swing.

The San Diego Swing Dance club has been around since 1970. It meets every Sunday 3-7pm at the El Cajon Elks Club with the first hour dedicated to teaching West Coast swing. The review or exposure to the basic steps helps new members transition quickly into the club's dance culture and helps expand club membership. Because many Swing club dancers have been dancing for some time, they are good. But a lot of younger dancers now populate the ranks because the music is contemporary and the moves are sexy. Many of the dancers, young and old, enjoy competing. I have watched dancers from eighteen to ninety compete.

The San Diego Swing Dance Club also boasts members who have been inducted into California's Dance Hall of Fame. Diane Lynn and Mary Manzella are both champions and standout dancers who have been inducted. Dancers of this caliber serve as instructors for new members and organize special workshops for the advanced dancers. Outings to counterpart clubs in Palm Spring, Long Beach and Los Angeles are arranged throughout the year. Bob Pomeroy, a long time member and club president, has been arranging joint club dances for years.

Innovations hosts a slightly younger dance crowd than the San Diego Swing Club. The club recently adopted a monthly rather than weekly dance featuring a top instructor. The new schedule and a well-known instructor are causing attendance figures to climb as well as revenue. Michael's Starlight studio is the site for Innovation dances.

Project Swing

The latest group activity in the West Coast arena is Parker Dearborn's Project Swing. This project is designed to expand the ranks of West Coast dancers throughout the San Diego area. Part of Michael Kiehm's teaching staff, Parker is also a nationally recognized champion and known across the country. Many of the best dancers in the area attend his classes and dance events. He also directs and choreographs Starlight's West Coast dance team.

Parker began his well-attended Project Swing event only recently. Starlight's parking lot is full every time a Project Swing event is scheduled. Michael John Kielbasa, another national champion and Michael Kiehm's nephew to boot, instructs both at Starlight and abroad. He also works closely with Parker in Project Swing events.

About a year ago, a film called "Lovin' Dancin'" was released. Although not a box office hit, it might be considered a cult movie for West Coast swing enthusiasts. Its story line involves the romantic entanglement of a couple competing in a West Coast swing event. But the appearance in that film of several top West Coast swing dancers turned it into mini documentary of West Coast swing. Seeing your heroes on film is always a delight to dance fans especially if you have taken classes from the leaders like Michael Kiehm, Jordan Frisbee, Parker Dearborn, Benji Schwimmer and Kyle Redd

As in most clubs, certain members are always at the core of things. For Innovations, individuals such as Mark Sheddon, Larry Armstrong, Debbie Dyar and Jill Curtis have been among the club's regulars. Mark, Larry and Jill are also certified West Coast swing instructors, certified by the master himself, Michael Kiehm.

Patty Wells, Champion Ballroom and Balboa Park

Patty Wells' dance center on Morena Blvd is close to the beach area and attracts sizeable crowds for Wednesday and Sunday night dance parties. The center offers a full range of dance instruction including West Coast swing.

Two other dance locations of note are the Champion Ballroom in Hillcrest and a Sunday night ballroom dance class in Balboa Park. Each has an excellent dance floor. Mary Murphy, a former judge on the popular "So You Think You Can Dance" TV program is the owner of the Champion Ballroom.

Humphrey's on Shelter Island occasionally features a blues band that attracts dancers. But its dance schedule varies and the dance floor is small.

Another out-of-town, dance spot popular with San Diego dancers is Top Cat located in an industrial park in Placentia in Orange County. It attracts enthusiastic dancers from Orange, Los Angeles and San Diego. The music is great, the crowd upbeat, and the dancing level high.

Like many West Coast devotees, I've enjoyed the influence of world class performers and instructors ranging from Michael Kiehm and his staff to Benji Schwimmer, Jordan Frisbee, Ben Morris, Arjay Centeno, Roy

Royston, Kyle Redd, Luis Crespo and Gary Jobst. Their female partners are just as exceptional adding beauty and remarkable grace. Tatiana Mollman, Sarah Vann Drake, Jessica Cox, Patty Vo and Dawn Kiehm are a few of the talented women who are standouts on the dance scene. They keep West Coast vibrant, growing, challenging and fun.

Intimate Getaways

Besides the dance clubs, there are smaller and more intimate getaways for West Coast swing devotees. Ciao Bella, a small Italian restaurant bar in La Mesa, was a favorite until its recent closure. Since then Tango del Rey, another dance setting with a comparable intimate atmosphere in the beach area has taken its place. Whenever a dance venue changes the word gets around quickly either by email, twitter or face book. Dancers from all over tend to drop in once they get the word. And, West Coasters have their own stable of DJs who ensure a continuous serving of the best west coast swing dance music.

For me, dancing is a source of continuous learning, physical exercise and enjoyment. Its gregariousness and sociability provide a unique exposure to America's cultural diversity. But the most enduring aspect is the influence of the many highly talented dancing masters and teachers, an influence that says be the best in whatever you undertake.

Chapter 9

SECOND DECADE AND BEYOND - 21st CENTURY

We begin the present decade with political upheavals across the Middle East, Africa and Southeast Asia, continuing economic challenges and continuing terrorist attacks. A massive earthquake racked Japan, a companion tsunami wreaked havoc on Japan's Fukushima nuclear plant, uprisings continue to plague the Arab world and domestic budget and employment woes continue to challenge the US. Before us lie years of efforts to rebuild our infrastructure, revamp our financial institutions, revisit our monetary policies and reinvent the way we govern ourselves.

Looking Back

For many years, I've had the opportunity to lead mostly senior groups in discussions featuring the most critical issues of the day. Most participants usually kept abreast of the news and welcomed an opportunity to share their views with others. These forums provided our seniors an opportunity for self-expression that too few citizens enjoy on a regular basis. Most of us are relegated to a passive posture of listening to talking heads and watching TV. But a moderated open discussion is an exhilarating experience and more influential than a passive listening posture.

We need more constructive dialogue; dialogue that is a stimulant to positive and productive action. Although we are not on the brink of a civil war, we do suffer from a political divide and institutional rules that stymie or slow efforts to improve the lot of our citizens. In his farewell address of 1796, George Washington warned against the spirit of parties. We saw the results of that early divide result in a bloody civil war. But philosophical divides are still with us to the frustration of a majority who would see us get on with the things that need doing. We must regain the sense of our common interests as Americans.

Too much time is squandered in Washington due to lack of statesmenship, negotiating skills and leadership. The US Supreme Court doesn't help matters when it hands down rulings in favor of big money in our election process. People wonder why it seems to take a catastrophe to galvanize us into action. The media would do us a great favor if they would focus our attention on the things that need doing – from potholes to energy. Journalists and the media have a great trust. They shape opinion and stimulate action.

Over the years, my forums have included topics ranging from the economy, education, health care and the infrastructure to inflation, commodity rigging, disaster management, compulsory national service, prison populations, term limits and weapons of mass destruction. Our considerations also include the disconnect between government and the public and the attitude towards the word freedom. For some freedom is interpreted as minimal interference by government in one's life and for others, freedom means the absence of want or fear. In either case, all consider freedom an essential element to pursuing one's dreams and aspirations.

The absence of a national master plan except for defense and emergencies may reflect America's federal-state division and separation of powers. Nevertheless the reach of the federal government from agriculture to the environment is undeniable. So too is the influence of strings accompanying federal dollars. While we are very good at laying out strategic visions for defense, plans for infrastructure continuity on a national and state-to-state basis go begging. We need a comprehensive domestic plan that is built with relevant state agency participation. This is a big job. Hopefully, such a plan would transcend conflicting ideology and politics. It would focus on things like high speed surface transit, new city and industrial locations, water and sewer systems, power grids, road networks and disaster management – things that are the legitimate province of government. Sometimes it is worthwhile reviewing the works of authors who have looked ahead and understand the waves of change. Two such books include Osborne and Gaebler's "Reinventing Government (1992) and Alvin and Heidi Toffler's "Creating a New Civilization"(1994).

Are we culturally averse to long range planning? It usually takes a cataclysmic event like Pearl Harbor, 9/11, or natural disaster to put us into a serious action mode. We seem to have trouble galvanizing action as long as the threat isn't imminent. Water is a case in point. Calfornia has endured drought conditions for years even though flanked by an ocean. Desalinization technology is now being applied but it has taken decades to arrive at this point. Financing for major construction projects has been the usual stumbling block. Issuing bonds for construction finance has saddled the State with enormous interest payouts. We need new financial tools to get on with needed tasks without the burden of high interest rates

New Retirees

You would think that America's new bumper crop of retirees would, after getting their fill of golf and grandkids, find an outlet for helping America respond to its challenges. Discussion groups like mine tend to attract those with a more activist mindset but more comparable discussion groups should be in action. Until more citizens have an outlet for speaking-up and being heard, progress on major fronts is likely to continue at a snail's pace. CSPAN does a great job in airing discussions on key issues by well-known figures. But many small discussion groups can fan the flames and force the hand of those in a position to make things happen.

The new longevity factor is now causing many to reassess their future. Armed with relatively good health and still sharp mentally, many seniors would welcome the opportunity of rejoin the excitement of the work world on their own terms. Many of their skills and knowledge stand the test of time and could benefit those younger tremendously. One area where the need is great and the physical demands minimal is education. The entry of senior Americans into the classroom could do wonders for the quality of teaching and the performance of our students.

I must admit that my earlier attempts to recruit retirees as paid teachers for my charter school were a dismal failure. Many retirees were either not interested or admitted to being burned out. Without doubt, there are limitations that come with aging. We may not move as fast and we may tire quicker. But in a computerized world, such limitations are hardly noticeable. And, for those where job demands are primarily intellectual, like teaching, longevity enhances rather than detracts. As most of my students are ready to admit, the stimulus of study and discussion has kept their minds in play in much the same manner that physical exercise aids the body.

As I frequently remind my students, discussions and opinions accomplish more than we think. In programs such as the Foreign Policy Associations' Great Decisions program, student opinions are routinely consolidated and sent to the White House, State Department and the Foreign Relations Committees of the House and Senate.

Projects Ahead

As for the future, I will likely continue doing much of what I have been doing but with some new twists. I would like to develop a number of different venues for World Affairs Forums and document the proceedings for wide distribution. Residential retirement-facilities, educational complexes and libraries will be targeted facilities.

I would also like to make a documentary on contemporary teaching methods in our middle schools and high schools. It would highlight how technology and the Internet and software, an environment in which students learn and develop the habit of self-teaching. The documentary would also highlight the teacher's role in guiding the student in content coverage, listening and speaking, taking notes and using the Internet.

My "to do" list also includes developing survey courses on political philosophy, education, US History and management. Of growing interest to me and others is the impact of technology and robotics on the workforce as well as the impact of boundary-less information processes on decision-making.

Job Creation

It has been obvious for some time that bold and imaginative planning is needed to overcome the job loss in this country. Private industry may be on the rebound but it is unlikely to absorb all the employees let go when the economy crashed – at least not until new industries and service needs emerge. Even then, the impact of computer driven systems and robotics will require new skill sets. Community colleges are assuming a key role in this transition. Government can also stimulate a significant number in jobs with infrastructure tasks such as high speed surface transit, the construct of new cities, the upgrade of water, power and sewer systems, bridge building and many other tasks. There is also the possibility of compulsory military service or other service in the public sector, more productive use of prison populations, and even the export of qualified people to assist underdeveloped nations in support of the Peace Corps and US Agency for International Development.

Schools

Developing better schools for our youth at least through high school is high on almost everyone's list. There are many different Charter schools that parents would like their children to attend were space or locations available. But leadership and facilities for these unique schools are not easy to come by. On campus modifications of traditional schools with staffing assist from retirees might be another way to go. A likely target for future charter sites in the San Diego area might include the Midway carrier museum and Marine and Navy installations.

Dancing

At present, my dancing interests center on West Coast swing and country western. There seems to be no end to the twists, turns and freestyle opportunities of West Coast swing which is why I like it so much. But every now and then, I see a Tango or English Quick Step being executed well and cast a fond eye in that direction.

Marine Corps Influence

The Marine Corps is noted for tradition and values. Proud of its heritage, Marines remind themselves of their scope of operations every time the Marines' hymn is sung - From the Halls of Montezuma to the Shores of Tripoli. As for values, the Marines cherish honor, courage and commitment. Marines are adamant in identifying with all who have served in their ranks. There is no such thing as an ex-Marine only former Marines. Clint Eastwood also highlighted other characteristic qualities of adaptation, improvisation and tenacity in his film entitled Heartbreak Ridge,

The Corps uses its museums to publicize its traditions and values. The museum at the San Diego Marine Recruit Depot is one of the finest west of the Mississipppi. Tours are hosted weekly by former Marines serving as docents. Each week a new company of Marine recruits are guided through the museum with the docents explaining the significance of the exhibits. The docents speak with authority since almost all have had first- hand experience connected with the artifacts on display. Far from static, the museum in constantly adding new exhibits and rearranging old. Changes and new additions are always in the works thanks to Barbara McCurtis, the museum director, and Pete Archuletea, the exhibit developer.

Recently while standing in front of a Korean exhibit featuring a large photo of a Marine machine gunner on a Korean hill. That gunner won the Navy Cross for his actions and is currently a museum docent. While looking at this exhibit, I was approached by one of the docents.

"Hi, my name is Joe Larkin. I take it you might have served in Korea?."

"Hi, Joe. I spent some time on the DMZ after the truce."

Following this conversation opener, Joe proceeded with some more questions that led to a remarkable discovery.

"Where did you enlist?"

"Philadelphia"

"What year?"

"51."

"What part of town did you live?"

"Germantown."

"What grammar school did you attend?

"Immaculate Conception"

"What did you say your name is?"

"Bob Byron"

There was a stunned silence for a moment. Then Joe smiled and added:

"Bobby Byron! We were classmates at Immaculate Conception. You and I used to play maneuvers when we were kids. Remember Sister So and So, Father So and So, Bill Merkle, Felix Longo, John LaVelle ? We've been looking for you for years. At our class reunions, you were the only one we could never account for"

The names of old school mates and the places we played in Germantown gushed out from us like a waterfall. Here we are some sixty-nine years later getting re-acquainted. And for the past few years, at least as long as my membership in the Marine Historical Society we had been passing each other like ships in the night. We have since made up for this long gap with recounts of our past at several local watering holes.

Anyone not acquainted with this story, gets an earful whenever they join us.

On most Friday mornings, a recruit graduation ceremony takes place on the MCRD parade deck complete with a marching band, a speech and awards. After a dismissal and a shout of Aye, Aye Sir, the new Marines take off for a brief leave before reporting to their first duty station. Whenever I feel the need of a Marine Corps "fix", I attend the ceremony and watch the flat-bellied new Marines and their Drill Instructors march. For a short time, I become a twenty-something again ready to report for duty. This is an organization I'll always be proud of having been part of. OORAA!!!

Everyman Accounting

Looking back on my programs, some were genuine standouts beginning with a program to redirect the careers of displaced engineers to high level consulting jobs in local government. Many found their way back to employment both in the public and private sectors but my follow-up proposal would have been the frosting on the cake.

That proposal involved the formation of a on-going think tank and consulting force serving local governments the same way we did in the original training program. It would have kept an amazingly versatile group of aerospace professionals intact. These individuals had already demonstrated their versatility. Savings resulting from improved operations and system streamlines would have more than defrayed the expenses of our organization. The concept remains as viable now as it was then.

A proposal to form a US Academy of Education would have given this country a real tool for improving educational quality across the land. A national level program would have prepared top high and college graduates for a mission to improve the US educational standing through continuous analysis of the best teaching practices world-wide. Like West Point or Annapolis, these students would earn their degrees while preparing for their mission. Graduates would be committed to serve for a specified time during which they would conduct global surveys, disseminate findings to American schools and help establish national academic standards. Although originally designed for the federal level, the academy could also function at the State level.

A variety of programs can be added to the list including those for Small Business Development, Computers for Kids, and a unique Gymkhana program. These programs were conducted in San Bernardino and Orange counties in conjunction with the Community Colleges in the area. The Small Business program included a segment focused on minority entrepreneurs. Computers for Kids took advantage of the momentum and enthusiasm created with the introduction of the Apple computer. Gymkhana introduced middle school students with their parents to an interdisciplinary world where the student's own body served as the laboratory for applied academics.

These were followed with business-related and history-oriented programs for the La Mesa-Spring Valley and Santee School districts. The La Mesa-Spring Valley program featured early morning team projects involving local businesses and government agencies. The Santee project provided a test run for the methods soon-to-be applied in a new Santee Explorer Academy charter school.

The next significant program was the founding and activation of the Santee Explorer Academy charter school. This was an aviation-oriented charter school that began at Gillespie Airfield in El Cajon. Plagued with facility problems only six months into its program, it did manage to introduce some new teaching concepts and made maximum use of the aerospace resources at Gillespie Airfield and nearby technology companies.

The Emeriti

Recently, I put in motion a program designed to reinforce the study of US history through eye witness accounts of historic events. Our first presentation involved the Cuban Missile Crisis of 1962. Our team, designated the Emeriti, consisted of a retired naval aviator Don

Hubbard, Bob McKenzie, an aide to Senator Tom Kuchel and myself, a management analyst working at General Dynamics on the Atlas Intercontinental Ballistic Missile program. Each presenter described their own role during these tense days of October and assessed lessons learned. These presentations were made to high school students in Coronado and Escondido as well as several community centers.

These presentations set the tone for future forays into the classrooms. San Diego has a sizeable veteran community and many are willing to share their experiences with students.

A To Do List

If I were to make an American "to do" list it would include the following: term limits for all public office holders including judges, a single payer health system that includes dental work, a minimal or no cost lifelong education system, universal military or public service for two years, income sufficient to enjoy life beyond the bare essentials, a foreign policy consistent with our domestic values, a solid infrastructure, a job for everyone who wants one, a vibrant middle class, simplification of our tax system, more productive use of prison populations, a national plebiscite when congress stalls and a re-evaluation of US monetary policy, banking systems and investment resources.

Meanwhile, the journey goes on. If the past is prologue, my future is spoken for – learning, teaching, dancing and related.

My family connections now stand at one daughter, four granddaughters and one son-in-law. My daughter Charlotte is an excellent mom. No one is as caring, devoted or hard working. She is also a nurse practitioner, has run her own clinic and has been managing and assisting her physician husband in their Pasadena office for years. Over the years, Charlotte has been a refuge in the storm on countless occasions for her mother, brother Mark, sisters Ginny and Robin and even her Dad. I feel remiss not visiting Charlotte and my granddaughters Aryn, Noor and Hanna more often. They live in La Canada just under a two hour drive from San Diego. Amber is a different story. She attends college in Sacramento.

I hope this book inspires readers to look back on their own lives. I've organized the recount of my journey in ten year increments. These increments seemed to fit naturally with activity segments of my own life. After chalking up enough mileage on your own life journey, you can get some idea of who you are; what you can do and cannot do. It also gives you some idea as to where you might be headed. For me, there is more I want to do. Besides, I'm doing what I love and, as noted in the beginning, that's a recipe for happiness.

Robert J. Byron

About the Author

Born in Philadelphia, educated in California, an officer in the Marine Corps, a designer of management and information systems for aerospace, a director of government and school activities, a faculty member of several community colleges whose dancing interests stimulated family cohesion and inspired a desire to excel in every undertaking.

His journey, now in its eighth decade, reflects both typical and atypical features of a life still in the making.

Index

F

G

N

T